Modular Programming with JavaScript

Modularize your JavaScript code for better readability, greater maintainability, and enhanced testability

Sasan Seydnejad

BIRMINGHAM - MUMBAI

Modular Programming with JavaScript

First published: July 2016

Production reference: 1150716

Published by Packt Publishing Ltd.
Livery Place
35 Livery Street
Birmingham B3 2PB, UK.

ISBN 978-1-78588-065-0

www.packtpub.com

Credits

Author
Sasan Seydnejad

Reviewer
Joe Dorocak
Muhammad Piracha

Commissioning Editor
Veena Pagare

Acquisition Editor
Smeet Thakkar

Content Development Editor
Mayur Pawanikar

Technical Editor
Anushree Arun Tendulkar

Copy Editor
Safis Editing

Project Coordinator
Nidhi Joshi

Proofreader
Safis Editing

Indexer
Mariammal Chettiyar

Graphics
Disha Haria

Production Coordinator
Nilesh Mohite

Cover Work
Nilesh Mohite

About the Author

Sasan Seydnejad has more than a decade of experience in web UI and frontend application development using JavaScript, CSS, and HTM in .NET and ASP.NET environments. He specializes in modular SPA design and implementation, responsive mobile-friendly user interfaces, AJAX, client architecture, and UX design, using HTML5, CSS3, and their related technologies. He implements framework-less and framework-based applications using Node.js, MongoDB, Express.js, and AngularJS. He is the holder of the U.S. patent for a user interface for a multi-dimensional data store — US Patent 6907428.

Writing this book has been an interesting journey and a lot of work but rewarding at the same time. I would like to thank my family who has always motivated me to learn and progress in my life as well as to help others along the way.

I would also like to thank my friends, my managers, my colleagues and all the other people who have been a positive influence in my life. You have helped me to grow personally and professionally.

Special thanks to my friend Taswar Bhatti for encouraging me to write this book and the book's Content Development Editor, Mayur Pawanikar for keeping me focused on the goal. Also, my book reviewers and all the people in PACKT publishing who made this book possible. My gratitude to JavaScript and open source community as a whole, thank you for your support through out the years.

About the Reviewer

Joe Dorocak, whose Internet moniker is Joe Codeswell, is a very experienced programmer. He enjoys creating readable code that implements the project requirements efficiently and understandably. He considers writing code akin to writing poetry.

Joe prides himself on the ability to communicate clearly and professionally. He considers his code to be a form of communication, not only with the machine platforms upon which it will run, but also with all the human programmers who will read it in the future.

Joe has been employed as a direct employee or a contractor by IBM, HP, GTE/Sprint, and other top-shelf companies. He is presently concentrating on the web app and web project consulting, coding primarily, but not exclusively, in Python and JavaScript. For more details, visit `https://www.linkedin.com/in/joedorocak`.

Muhammad Piracha is director of engineering at Bamboo Solutions Corporation, based in Reston, Virginia. Bamboo Solutions is a leading provider of software solutions for the Microsoft® SharePoint® platform. Muhammad has over 18 years experience building document management software applications using various Microsoft products.

Currently he oversees several teams across engineering, research and quality assurance to constantly improve the existing portfolio of over 50 products. He is a major driving force in helping the company to develop strategy, architecture, and direction for new initiatives in the SharePoint Online and Office 365™ space.

www.PacktPub.com

eBooks, discount offers, and more

Did you know that Packt offers eBook versions of every book published, with PDF and ePub files available? You can upgrade to the eBook version at www.PacktPub.com and as a print book customer, you are entitled to a discount on the eBook copy. Get in touch with us at customercare@packtpub.com for more details.

At www.PacktPub.com, you can also read a collection of free technical articles, sign up for a range of free newsletters and receive exclusive discounts and offers on Packt books and eBooks.

https://www2.packtpub.com/books/subscription/packtlib

Do you need instant solutions to your IT questions? PacktLib is Packt's online digital book library. Here, you can search, access, and read Packt's entire library of books.

Why subscribe?

- Fully searchable across every book published by Packt
- Copy and paste, print, and bookmark content
- On demand and accessible via a web browser

Table of Contents

Preface

There are many JavaScript books on the market these days, and some of them are very good. However, most of them focus on various aspects of the language itself or using certain frameworks to build JavaScript applications. In this book, we are going to take a different approach and look at the architectural design of creating JavaScript applications based on modules, without the need for third-party frameworks.

Creating a good application is more than just writing good code, it is also about how different pieces of the application work and interact with each other. Another characteristic of a good application is its ability to be easily maintained, scaled and extended as needed. A proper modular design enables us to achieve all such goals in our application seamlessly.

In the beginning of this book, I'll be introducing you to the fundamentals of JavaScript modules and the concepts behind a good modular design. Leveraging these concepts, we'll be building an application together, step-by-step, so we can apply what we learn in practice. I recommend reading the chapters in the sequence that they are presented so you can follow along with ease and observe how our design evolves over time.

I would very much encourage you to develop the application pieces with me, as the intent of this book is to be very hands-on, and I would like you to feel as a member of the development team for this application.

As in the real world, we will be re-factoring our code-base a few times during the development phase, in order to implement the new concepts as they are introduced and improve the quality of our application.

Keep in mind that we will be creating a client-side application, and as such, there is no server-side code involved. Nonetheless, many concepts that we will be covering regarding modules and modular architecture can be applied to server-side applications too.

Also, as this book is an introduction to modular JavaScript application design, we will develop a Proof of concept (POC)-grade application together which can provide a good starting point for your own projects.

I have taken a minimalist approach in the implementation, and as a result, we will be using very few third-party libraries in our development process. Therefore, instead of focusing on studying new libraries and how to work with them, you can focus on the application's architecture instead. Once we create a solid foundation, we can incorporate other libraries into our design as required.

For the purposes of clarity, I have shied away from writing fancy code, so you don't have to spend much time trying to understand the intricacies of the code, as opposed to the big picture and how the pieces fit and work together.

Note that this book is meant for people who have a good understanding of JavaScript language, but would like to learn more about JavaScript client-side application design. If you find yourself having trouble with the language itself, you can always refer to online resources and the JavaScript community. This community consists of many smart and helpful people who can, and will be willing to answer your questions. I, for one, am very grateful to the community for its help in my professional growth over the years.

I hope you'll find the book informative and by seeing the benefits of a modular architecture, will use the concepts presented in this book in your own future projects.

What this book covers

Chapter 1, What Are Modules and Their Advantages?, introduces you to the concept of modules and how they can help us design a robust and scalable application.

Chapter 2, Review of Important JavaScript OOP Concepts, covers an overview of some of the important OOP concepts in JavaScript which are necessary for the design and implementation of the modules in our application.

Chapter 3, Module Design Pattern, introduces a very common pattern in creating modules in JavaScript and shows how this pattern can be implemented.

Chapter 4, Designing Simple Modules, uses the module pattern to create simple modules which work together to form the building blocks of our application.

Chapter 5, Module Augmentation, shows the use of various techniques to add more functionality to our modules so that we can extend their capabilities further.

Chapter 6, Cloning, Inheritance, and Submodules, covers how to create modules based on other modules in our application, as well as some more techniques to enhance our modules.

Chapter 7, Base, Sandbox, and Core Modules, introduces some of the main pieces of our application and demonstrates how to create loose coupling among our application modules.

Chapter 8, Application Implementation – Putting It All Together, shows us how to apply all the concepts that we have learned regarding modular architectural design, in order to implement all the pieces of our application.

Chapter 9, Modular Application Design and Testing, covers how to test our application modules using either plain JavaScript or third-party frameworks.

Chapter 10, Enterprise Grade Modular Design, AMD, CommonJS, and ES6 Modules, introduces different modular formats in JavaScript which can be used to design modules, as well as how modules can be imported and exported in our application using these formats.

What you need for this book

You will require any modern browser (IE 9+, Chrome, Safari, Firefox) and any OS that can run a modern browser from the preceding list.

The third-party library required would be jQuery 1.8+.

For the later chapters, the following are the third-party libraries:

- Jasmin 2+
- Mocha (latest version)
- Chai (latest version)
- RequireJS (latest version)

Who this book is for

If you are an intermediate to advanced JavaScript developer who has an experience of writing JavaScript code, but probably not in a modular portable manner, or you are looking to develop enterprise-level JavaScript applications, then this book is for you.

A basic understanding of JavaScript concepts such as OOP, prototypal inheritance, and closures is expected.

Conventions

In this book, you will find a number of text styles that distinguish between different kinds of information. Here are some examples of these styles and an explanation of their meaning.

Code words in text, database table names, folder names, filenames, file extensions, pathnames, dummy URLs, user input, and Twitter handles are shown as follows: "Notice that I have created a function and called it `MyObjDefinition`".

A block of code is set as follows:

```
function doAddition(num1, num2){
   return num1 + num2;
}
```

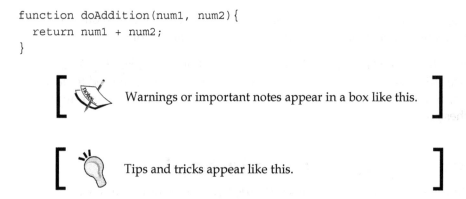

Warnings or important notes appear in a box like this.

Tips and tricks appear like this.

Reader feedback

Feedback from our readers is always welcome. Let us know what you think about this book—what you liked or disliked. Reader feedback is important for us as it helps us develop titles that you will really get the most out of.

To send us general feedback, simply e-mail `feedback@packtpub.com`, and mention the book's title in the subject of your message.

If there is a topic that you have expertise in and you are interested in either writing or contributing to a book, see our author guide at `www.packtpub.com/authors`.

Customer support

Now that you are the proud owner of a Packt book, we have a number of things to help you to get the most from your purchase.

Downloading the example code

You can download the example code files for this book from your account at
`http://www.packtpub.com`. If you purchased this book elsewhere, you can
visit `http://www.packtpub.com/support` and register to have the files e-mailed
directly to you.

You can download the code files by following these steps:

1. Log in or register to our website using your e-mail address and password.
2. Hover the mouse pointer on the **SUPPORT** tab at the top.
3. Click on **Code Downloads & Errata**.
4. Enter the name of the book in the **Search** box.
5. Select the book for which you're looking to download the code files.
6. Choose from the drop-down menu where you purchased this book from.
7. Click on **Code Download**.

You can also download the code files by clicking on the **Code Files** button on the
book's webpage at the Packt Publishing website. This page can be accessed by
entering the book's name in the **Search** box. Please note that you need to be logged in
to your Packt account.

Once the file is downloaded, please make sure that you unzip or extract the folder
using the latest version of:

- WinRAR / 7-Zip for Windows
- Zipeg / iZip / UnRarX for Mac
- 7-Zip / PeaZip for Linux

The code bundle for the book is also hosted on GitHub at `https://github.com/`
`PacktPublishing/ModularProgrammingwithJavaScript`. We also have other code
bundles from our rich catalog of books and videos available at `https://github.`
`com/PacktPublishing/`. Check them out!

Errata

Although we have taken every care to ensure the accuracy of our content, mistakes do happen. If you find a mistake in one of our books—maybe a mistake in the text or the code—we would be grateful if you could report this to us. By doing so, you can save other readers from frustration and help us improve subsequent versions of this book. If you find any errata, please report them by visiting http://www.packtpub.com/submit-errata, selecting your book, clicking on the **Errata Submission Form** link, and entering the details of your errata. Once your errata are verified, your submission will be accepted and the errata will be uploaded to our website or added to any list of existing errata under the Errata section of that title.

To view the previously submitted errata, go to https://www.packtpub.com/books/content/support and enter the name of the book in the search field. The required information will appear under the **Errata** section.

Piracy

Piracy of copyrighted material on the Internet is an ongoing problem across all media. At Packt, we take the protection of our copyright and licenses very seriously. If you come across any illegal copies of our works in any form on the Internet, please provide us with the location address or website name immediately so that we can pursue a remedy.

Please contact us at copyright@packtpub.com with a link to the suspected pirated material.

We appreciate your help in protecting our authors and our ability to bring you valuable content.

Questions

If you have a problem with any aspect of this book, you can contact us at questions@packtpub.com, and we will do our best to address the problem.

1
What Are Modules and Their Advantages?

In this very first chapter, I will provide you with an overview of the modular design approach in application development as it relates to JavaScript applications.

I will also mention parallels between the modular style of application architecture and the real-life examples of this conceptual design.

Hopefully, as you read along, you'll be able to relate to at least some aspects of the modular design approach and start to see why this style of organizing your code can be extremely beneficial.

The main objective of this chapter is to create a familiar context for you, and to get you started on thinking the modular way as you create and organize your code. Soon, you will see that this approach can organically grow into a well-defined application architecture methodology.

We will start the chapter with a brief discussion on how we can organize our code based on specialization. Then we will look at how we can define modules based on the functionality that they provide.

The topics that are covered in this chapter are:

- The simple rule to creating modules
- A real life example of modules
- A look at a non-modular example
- Re-factoring into a more modular approach
- Designing in a modular way

Prelude to modular programming

Many years ago, when I was taking my first computer programming course at college, I found myself having having difficulty organizing organizing my code into functions and classes. I always wondered what kind of criteria I needed to keep in mind to qualify a chunk of code to belong to a function or to a class or a subclass. When should I break down one function into multiple functions or a class into multiple classes?

Of course, there were some rules and guidelines that I was familiar with such as "a function should not be too long or should not do too many things; a class should be a blueprint of a data type" and so on. However, such rules and guidelines seemed abstract to me and I wanted to find a rule that was precise and applicable in all situations.

As I became more knowledgeable in programming concepts and gained more experience in application design, I was able to write more sophisticated code and organize my code better into functions and classes.

However, while my code was organized into well-defined functions and classes, such functions and classes still seemed scattered in different parts of the application. When I needed to make modifications to one piece of the application, I would be concerned about the impact that the change would have on other pieces and the functionality of the application as a whole.

As my applications grew larger and became more complex, the impact of the changes and enhancements became even more pronounced. There were more things things that could adversely affect the application if the application pieces were not designed properly.

Browser-based applications were particularly vulnerable to such impacts as different parts of the application could be manipulating the same element in the browser, which would produce unexpected behaviors and effects in other parts of the application.

On the other hand, making small changes to the application was a challenge on its own, as finding the best place to make such small changes was not always very obvious. Each piece of the application could be performing many different activities from manipulation DOM to writing to cookie to making AJAX calls.

What if I could make one part of the application responsible for only one type of functionality? What if only one part of the application was responsible for all cookie-related functionality? What if only one piece would make AJAX calls to the server and provide the other pieces of the application with the returned data?

As we design functions and classes to specialize in doing very specific tasks, we can also bundle such functions and classes together to act as a specialized piece of the application responsible for providing one particular functionality. The key point here is to create specialized code packages.

This would mean that changes in how we read and write to cookies would only take place in the package that is responsible for cookie operations and such changes would have no impact on how AJAX calls are made to the server.

If we organize our code into specialized packages, (or modules as we will call them) we can easily achieve this goal of separation of concerns and responsibilities among our application pieces.

But before we can organize our code into modules, we need to see how we decide that a chunk of code should be a module.

The simple rule for creating modules

I need to emphasize on the fact that modular programming is not some magical and mystical design concept and pattern that is hard to grasp and even harder to implement. It is really just a practical approach to organizing our code in such a way that each chunk of code only does a very specific and specialized task.

The idea is that each module is a loosely coupled piece of the application, a building block that, along with other pieces (and other modules), creates an ecosystem, that is your application.

So here is the simple rule for creating modules: "If a piece of your application provides a specialized functionality, it can be made into a module that can also be reused in other applications."

I mentioned previously that I was looking for a "precise" rule to help me organize my application code but as my experience has shown, there is no such precise rule other than what I mentioned above, which is in fact not a rule but a guideline. And as a guideline, there is flexibility in what can be considered a module or not. This can be best decided both at the design time and as the application evolves since the application needs can change over time.

A real-life example of modules

Let's consider a familiar modular system. You are most likely reading this book in a place that has electricity and there are many electric outlets in the walls surrounding you. This system enables you to plug in various electrical devices into the outlets and each one of these devices is designed to do a very specific task.

Consider the electrical devices that are plugged into some of these outlets: microwaves, electric kettles, washers, dryers, and so on.

None of these devices care if they are plugged into the electrical outlet in your house or your neighbor's house. They are designed to do their specific task and functionality when they are plugged in and when the power is on, regardless of whose house they are in.

Our application modules should follow the same philosophy. This means, regardless of where in the application they are plugged in and even regardless of what application they are plugged into, they should do their specific task and only their specific task.

Also, in exactly the same way that an electrical device can easily be unplugged from the wall outlet, a code module should be designed in such a way that it can easily be decoupled and removed from your application.

Furthermore, as the removal of one electrical device has no impact on the functionality of other devices that are plugged into your electrical system, the removal of a code module or a series of code modules from your application should not have any effect on the functionality of the other parts of your application.

This decoupling should also have no effect on the application as a whole, other than perhaps just losing the specific functionality that was provided by that particular module or group of modules in your application.

In this book, we will explore how creating modules will help in designing better specialized code pieces that can easily be plugged into and unplugged from our applications. We will also see how modular architecture provides for a more robust and flexible application as a whole.

We will discover how this kind of architectural approach leads to huge advantages in many aspects of our application fundamentals such as code usability, maintainability, testability, and many more.

I hope now you are curious enough to at least consider modular programming in general and JavaScript modular programming in particular as a possible approach for your future application design.

In further chapters, we will apply the same principles that we discussed regarding electrical outlets and appliances to our code modules, in both the design and implementation phases.

A look at a non-modular example

Let's consider an extremely simple example and see how the (somehow) **specialized** modular approach differs from a non-modular one.

We start by writing a couple of functions in the traditional way, as following:

```
function doAddition(num1, num2){
  return num1 + num2;
}

function doSubtraction(num1, num2){
  var result = null;
  if(num1 > num2){
  result = num1 - num2;

  }else{
    result = num2 - num1;
  }
  return result;
}

console.log(doAddition(3,2)); // displays 5

console.log(doSubtraction(3,2)); // displays 1
```

As you can see in the above code, we have two independent functions for doing simple additions and subtractions and there is no relation between the two, other than the fact that they both operate on the two passed-in numbers (numeric values).

If we had implemented these functions in an application and were to do the identical operations in a different application, we most likely would either rewrite the same functions in that application from scratch or we would copy/paste the code from this application into the other one.

What if we now decided to also do multiplication, division, and other related calculations in our application using the same approach?

Well, one way would be to just continue writing independent functions as above and add them to our application. This approach could work and would get the job done, but probably not in the best way, since as the code grows it will become more disorganized and chaotic.

By using this approach, not only would we be polluting the global namespace with a bunch of global functions that could possibly collide with other global functions of the same name. We would also end up with scattered pieces of code that had not been packaged together based on their functionality and specialization.

If all such functions do mathematical calculations of one kind or another and that is the commonality that they all have, how about if we create a **package** (module) that specializes in mathematical calculations?

This would allow us to have a specialized package that regardless of the application that it is hosted in, would always provide the same specialized functionality.

Let's even imagine a step further and assume that we created this package in a separate JavaScript file that can be added as an independent module to any application.

Even better, how about if this module only would get added (requested from the server, in the case of a client side web application) to the application at runtime, and only when needed?

This type of implementation would give us the ability to load chunks, pieces, or modules of the code when needed at runtime and then unload them when the application does not need them anymore. This would enable us to cut down on the footprint of our application on the client side while providing all the necessary functionality as needed and on demand.

Such an approach can also be very useful on mobile devices which have limited bandwidth and resources to be leveraged.

Rest assured that I do intend to explore all such possibilities with you in the later chapters of this book.

Re-factoring to a more modularized approach

Let's consider re-factoring the two functions that we looked at previously and putting them together in a more specialized package (class or module) called, CalculationHandler, as shown below:

```
function CalculationHandler(){
  CalculationHandler.result = null;
}

CalculationHandler.doAddition = function(num1, num2){
  return num1 + num2;
};

CalculationHandler.doSubtraction = function(num1, num2){
```

```
    if(num1 > num2){
      CalculationHandler.result = num1 - num2;

    }else{
      CalculationHandler.result = num2 - num1;
    }
    return CalculationHandler.result;

  };

  console.log(CalculationHandler.doAddition(3,2)); // displays 5
  console.log(CalculationHandler.doSubtraction(3,2)); // displays 1
```

As you can see in this "module" (and I use the term loosely here; you will see why in later chapters), I am using a function object and adding properties (methods) to this object. This methods do specialized tasks related to the overall functionality of the object (module), such as addition and subtraction.

A note about our module here

If you are more experienced in JavaScript programming, you are probably thinking that the way I have created this module is probably not the best way to create a real module in JavaScript, and you are right! But for now, the big idea here is that any piece of code that does a specialized task can be tagged as a module, for the most part.

However, there are certainly better ways to write more robust and extensible modules in JavaScript. For instance, creating a module can be accomplished much better by using the **Module Design Pattern**, which we will get to explore a lot further in later chapters of this book.

Designing in a modular way

In the early stages of designing an application, one of the most important steps is to decide on the functionality that the application needs to provide. This of course, is based on the overall purpose of the application and the type of application that you are designing.

Based on such requirements, in the design phase, you should try to break down the overall functionality (the big picture) of the application into smaller and specialized pieces. Then, you can determine if such pieces already exist, either in the form of third-party libraries or the code that you have already written for a different application.

If you already have your own chunks of reusable code designed in a modular fashion (most third-party libraries are designed in such a way too), it would be much easier and quicker to connect these pieces together and use them in your new application. This would be the same as putting various Lego blocks together to create a play structure.

This type of approach is very important and fits quite well within an **Agile** development environment. This enables you to work on well defined, specialized modules as you need them and as new application requirements are defined. Also, as you create your code based on modules, you are able to prevent tight coupling among your application pieces.

On the other hand, this approach allows different developers to work on different pieces (modules) of the same application, independently of each other. Another advantage is that modules can be tested separately and in different environments before being added to the application.

In time and with more experience in modular application design and implementation, you will become better at deciding how to distinguish and design your modules. However, it is not realistic to think you can come up with the complete list of all the modules that you could ever need in your application, in the first attempt.

That is because applications evolve and requirements change over time. You may need to create new modules, or modify current ones, or decide to use a different module or library altogether to accommodate such changes in the requirements.

The key advantage of modular design is the flexibility that is provides. Dealing with all the situations mentioned above is a lot easier and requires a lot less effort in a modular architecture. It will also mitigate the impact that adding, removing, or modifying a module could possibly have on the application as a whole.

In the following chapters, you will see how we can create simple and complex modules and how they will be added to our application as loosely coupled pieces.

You will also see how we can load such modules dynamically and on demand when we need them in our application.

So, let's get ready for an exciting journey into our future application design, using modular architecture.

Summary

In this chapter, we tried to get an overview of the concepts behind modular programming in general and how such concepts can be used in JavaScript applications in particular.

We saw that this approach is essentially based on creating packages of specialized code that do very specific tasks.

We also made parallels between how modules are designed in real life and our application modules, so that we can translate the similarities into our own application design approach.

While the term "module" can be used to refer to different things in the code, we will take this terminology to refer to a certain style of programming and architecture in our JavaScript application design approach in later chapters.

However, before we completely dive into the more technical aspects of JavaScript modular programming, it is a good idea to review the fundamentals of object-oriented programming in JavaScript in the next chapter. This will allow us to establish a solid foundation for more technical chapters as we move forward.

2
Review of Important JavaScript OOP Concepts

Before we start creating and using our modules in JavaScript, it is important to have a good grasp of important **Object Oriented Programming (OOP)** concepts in JavaScript. We will rely on such concepts to design and implement our application modules in later chapter.

While my intent in this chapter is not to explore such conceptes in great depth, I will try to provide a good overview of some of the most important related topics.

If you feel that you are quite familiar with these concepts in JavaScript, you could skip this chapter and move on to the next one.

However, if you are not very familiar with OOP in JavaScript, even if you are familiar with similar concepts in classical object oriented languages, I encourage you to follow along as things are a little different in JavaScript. I think it will be worthwhile for you to have a look at these concepts in the realm of JavaScript.

In this chapter, we will cover:

- JavaScript objects and their constructors
- What `this` keyword is and how it behaves in different contexts
- Closure and its uses
- Inheritance in JavaScript
- Prototype chaining

And other related topics.

JavaScript objects

If you have programmed in JavaScript before (as I'm sure you have, since this book is intended for intermediate to advanced JavaScript programmers), you will certainly have used objects, even if you have not been aware of their inner workings.

If you are familiar with other more classical object oriented languages (such as C++, C#, or Java), you'll be surprised to know that there is no formal syntax for defining classes in JavaScript (at least till **ECMAScript 6**). I think you'll be even more surprised to find out that, without having a formal syntax, you are still able to create classes in JavaScript and harness the full power of object oriented design and architecture (and one could even argue in a more flexible way).

> **Formal class definition in JavaScript**
>
> In the newer version of JavaScript (ES6), new syntax allows you to define classes in a more formal and structured way.
>
> For more information visit the following link:
>
> `http://es6-features.org/`

You can create objects in JavaScript in many different ways but we will focus on three of these approaches for creating objects in this chapter. These approaches are:

* Using native object type constructors
* Using object literal notation
* Using constructor functions

Object type constructors

Probably the easiest way to create objects in JavaScript is to create an instance of the Object type and then augment it with properties that we need.

As you might know, the Object type is the top level object (the root object) in JavaScript that all other objects are created from behind the scenes. This object has many properties which have been defined for it by default. Every object created based on this type will inherit these default properties such as `toString`, `valueOf`, `hasOwnProperty`, and so on.

Have a look at the following syntax as it shows the creation of an object using the `Object` constructor and augmenting it with custom properties:

```
var myObj = new Object();

myObj.value = "my first value";
myObj.method = function(){
```

```
    return this.value;
};


console.log(myObj.method()); // displays "my first value"
```

This syntax for creating objects was very popular at one point. However, it is no longer used as much, since using other methods of creating objects allows for a better conceptual view of how the object properties are packaged. Also, using an object constructor is not as optimized, since the interpreter needs to do a scope resolution to determine whether there is a local constructor with the same name or not, in order to create the scope chain properly.

> **Regarding scope chains**
>
> A **scope chain** is a chain of objects whose properties are looked for when looking for the existence and value of a property.
>
> For more information visit the following link:
>
> https://blogs.msdn.microsoft.com/jscript/2007/07/26/ scope-chain-of-jscript-functions/

Object literal notation

Creating objects using **object literal notation** allows for a good conceptual view of the object and all of its properties.

This approach is also very popular for passing multiple parameters to functions instead of passing one parameter at a time. This method of passing parameters allows us to package all the parameters neatly into an object (usually as an anonymous object) and pass it as one parameter into the function.

Using this syntax, an object in JavaScript can be created as simply as shown here:

```
var obj = {};
```

Of course, this object does not do anything and is completely useless, but nonetheless it is a valid object (**Singleton**).

Let's create another object using this approach, as shown here:

```
var MyFirstObj = {
  myFirstValue : 2,
  mySecondValue : 5,

  addValues: function(){
    return this.myFirstValue + this.mySecondValue ;
  }
};
```

In the code above, we have created a variable that has been initialized with an object. Our object here consists of two value properties and a simple method (method property) to add these value properties.

To interact with the object in the preceding code, we can use the variable that holds (references) the object MyfirstObj and access its members using the dot notation, as follows:

```
console.log( MyFirstObj.addValues()); // displays 7
```

Function objects

In JavaScript, functions are considered first class objects. In fact, anytime you are dealing with a function, you are dealing with an object.

We do not always use functions as objects in JavaScript but, when are used as objects, we can use them as constructors to create other objects.

Functions as object constructors (classes)

Let's mimic the object definition in the previous section, which was written as an object literal, and create a constructor function to achieve the same functionality. Consider the following:

```
function MyObjDefinition(){
   var myFirstValue = 2;
   var mySecondValue = 5;

   this.addValues = function(){
      return myFirstValue + mySecondValue;
   };
}

var myFirstObj = new MyObjDefinition();

console.log( myFirstObj.addValues()); // displays 7
```

Notice that I have created a function and called it MyObjDefinition. I named the function as such to indicate that this function is going to be used as a definition (class) to create other objects from.

Using the new keyword, we can create an instance of this object and assign it to the myFirstObj variable.

If you are not used to using function objects as constructors, at this point you might wonder if MyObjDefinition is a function, a class, or an object?

Well, MyObjDefinition is all of those! I will explain this in more depth shortly.

Functions as static objects

Let's modify the preceding code so we can see how MyObjDefinition can be better thought of as an object.

```
// defining an object
function MyObjDefinition(){
  MyObjDefinition.myFirstValue = 2;
  MyObjDefinition.mySecondValue = 5;
}

// adding a property to the object
MyObjDefinition.addValues = function(){

  return this.myFirstValue + this.mySecondValue;
};

// initializing the object by calling it
   as a function
MyObjDefinition();
```

As you can see, we have moved our inner addValues method to the outside of the object definition and used the dot notation to add it to MyObjDefinition object as a property.

The reason that we can use such syntax is because JavaScript considers MyObjDefinition function as both a function and an object. Since we can assign properties to objects dynamically in JavaScript, we are able to assign the addValues function as a property to this object, using the dot notation.

Note that we have called our object definition as a regular function to initialize the default values for the myFirstValue and mySecondValue properties. Of course, we can do this because MyObjDefinition is also a function.

We also have changed the myFirstValue and mySecondValue variables inside the function definition to MyObjDefinition.myFirstValue and MyObjDefinition. mySecondValue, respectively. This is so MyObjDefinition.addValues can access them from outside the function definition. If you are not sure what this keyword is, do not be concerned as we will talk about it shortly.

To add the two values, we can still use the same syntax as before:

```
console.log( MyObjDefinition.addValues()); // displays 7
```

Notice that we are not able to use MyObjDefinition as a constructor function as we did before, since now it is acting as a static object. So the following will produce an error:

```
var anotherObj = new MyObjDefinition();
anotherObj.addValues(); // error
```

In this scenario, while we are creating an object using the new keyword, the created object does not have the properties of the MyObjDefinition function.

This exercise in re-factoring of our code shows how functions can act as function as well as objects in JavaScript, depending on the usage.

I like the flexibility that JavaScript offers in how objects can be defined, as well as how dynamic properties can be added to objects as needed. However, I can see why some programmers with a background in more classical object oriented languages might find the approach a little confusing.

My take on the subject is that JavaScript has its own realm and it is best to understand it within its realm, as opposed to trying to see it in the context of classical object oriented languages.

Object literal notation versus function objects

While both object literal notation and function object syntax can be used to create objects, there are situations when one approach is better suited than the other.

In JavaScript, after the script is parsed, all the function declarations in the program are hoisted to the beginning of the script. That is why you can call a function before its actual definition in the code, as shown in the following example:

```
var firstPerson = CreatePerson("Tom", "Software Developer");

function CreatePerson(personName, personJob){
   // creating an object instance, using object type
   var person = new Object();
   // we can also use an object literal instead as below
   // var person = {};
   person.name = personName;
   person.job = personJob;
```

```
    return person;
}

console.log(firstPerson.name); // displays "Tom"
```

In the preceding code, every time `CreatePerson` function is called a new object is created, augmented, and then returned. This approach is also known as the **Object Factory** design pattern.

> **Design patterns in JavaScript**
>
> If you are not familiar with design patterns in general or would like to become more familiar with design patterns in JavaScript, I highly recommend the following resource:
>
> *Mastering JavaScript Design Patterns, Simon Timms.*

Notice that the call to the `CreatePerson` function is taking place before the actual function definition. This code will not generate an error when it is run because of function hoisting. Behind the scenes, the function `CreatePerson` has been hoisted to the top of the script so when the call is made to this function, the declaration has already been encountered by the interpreter.

Because of this mechanism, you don't have to worry if the call to the function takes place before the function declaration or not.

This does not apply to object literals since there are no function declarations and, thus, no hoisting involved. Therefore, all the calls to such objects need to happen AFTER the object definition.

Consider the following example:

```
var Tom = {
  name: "Tom"
};
Tom.job = "SoftWare Developer";

console.log(Tom.job); // displays "Software Developer"
console.log(Tom.name); // displays "Tom"
```

Here, we are first defining an object, using object literal notation, and then adding a property to it. Everything works fine and as expected.

However, if we try to add a property to this object before the object definition, as follows:

```
Tom.job = "SoftWare Developer"; // "TypeError: Cannot set property
'job' of undefined"

var Tom = {
  name: "Tom"
};
```

We will encounter an error.

You may also have noticed that, in the case of constructor functions, the `Person` function in our example, we can pass arguments to the constructor and create different instances of `Person` with different names and different job titles. However, this cannot be done when using object literal notation to create objects.

As you can tell by now, these different approaches for creating objects are suited for different purposes. Most of the time, we use constructor functions when we need to create multiple instances of an object but use object literal notation to package parameters (data) that need to be passed to different parts of the application.

Objects created using object literal notation are also best suited for creating modular code, which we will see a whole lot more of later in the upcoming chapters.

Let's make things a little more interesting and re-factor the preceding code so we can use both approaches to creating objects together.

Have a look at the following:

```
function CreatePerson(personData){
  var person = {}; // using Object literal
  person.name = personData.Name;
  person.job = personData.Job;

  return person;
}

var personData = {
  Name: "Tom",
  Job: "Software Developer"
};

var firstPerson = new CreatePerson(personData);

console.log(firstPerson.name); // displays "Tom"
```

Here, we are using object literal notation to create a person data object (`personData`) and then pass this data object as a package to the `CreatePerson` constructor to create our `firstPerson` instance.

In the chapters ahead, we will be using both of these object creation approaches to create our modules.

The "this" keyword

You saw an example of using the `this` keyword when we looked at our static object in this chapter. We will now spend some time on `this` to understand what it is and how it can help us write better code.

The `this` keyword is simply a reference to an object. However, that reference can point to different objects at different times, depending on the code execution context.

To see what that means, let's start by creating a simple constructor function:

```
function Person(){
   this.name = "Tom";
   this.job = "Software Developer";
}
```

In the preceding code, the `this` keyword has a global context. So inside the `Person` function, `this` refers to the `window` object (if the code is run in a browser). In fact, if we execute the following:

```
Person();
```

We have now created two properties for the `window` object, called `name` and `job`. We can prove this by running the following:

```
console.log(window.name); // displays "Tom";
console.log(window.job); // displays "Software Developer";
```

Keep in mind that adding properties to the global context (the `window` object) is not a good idea and will pollute the global context as well as creating a high possibility of naming collisions. This could result in unexpected behavior in the code and strange bugs that are hard to track.

But the `this` keyword can take a whole new context and reference a totally different object, when used as the following:

```
function CreatePerson(personData){
   this.name = personData.Name;
   this.job = personData.Job;
```

```
    }

    var personOneData = {
      Name: "Tom",
      Job: "Software Developer"
    };

    var firstPerson = new CreatePerson(personOneData);

    console.log(firstPerson.name);// displays "Tom"
    console.log(firstPerson.job); // displays "Software Developer"
```

Here, we are creating a new person object using our `CreatePerson` constructor. By using the `new` keyword, an instance of person is created and the variable `firstPerson` now holds a reference to this instance. This person instance has its `name` property set to `Tom` and its `job` property to `Software Developer`.

Note that the `this` keyword inside this object now refers to the instance.

Let's create another person object definition as below:

```
    var personTwoData = {
      Name: "John",
      Job: "Software Architect"
    };
```

And use our constructor function to create an instance of this second person.

Once the following code is executed, `this` will refer to the instance of this second person.

```
    var secondPerson = new CreatePerson(personTwoData);
```

We can examine the properties of the second person, as follows:

```
    console.log(secondPerson.name); // displays "John";
    console.log(secondPerson.job); // displays "Software Architect"
```

Things can get a little more interesting at times and a bit harder to figure out what the context of `this` can be in different circumstances.

Consider the following example:

```
    var name = "The window global";

    var myOwnObject = {
```

```
    name: "my Own Object",

  getName: function(){
    return this.name;
  }
};
```

As you can see in this example, we have defined an object using object literal notation. This object is assigned to the `myOwnObject` variable and its `getName` method returns the value of the `name` property in the object. So, as you might expect, `this` in this context refers to the context of `myOwnObject`:

```
console.log(myOwnObject.getName()); // displays "my Own Object"
```

However, if we make an assignment such as:

```
// displays "The Window global"
console.log((myOwnObject.getName = myOwnObject.getName)());
```

This will produce the result: **The window global**. This result is rather confusing.

When we make the above assignment, only the function gets assigned from the left side of the expression to the right side of the expression and now `this` refers to the global object. Note that, in this scenario, `myOwnObject.getName` is just a function and as explained before `this` inside a function (not an instance of an object) always refers to the global context, which produces the result, **The window global**, when executed in the browser.

Let's consider another object definition and create an inner function (a **Closure**, which we will talk about shortly) inside this object. The context of `this` may not be what you expect in this scenario.

```
var name = "The window global";
var myOwnObject = {

  name: "my Own Object",
  getName: function(){
    return function(){
      return this.name;
    };
  }
};

console.log(myOwnObject.getName()()); // displays "The window global"
```

Since the innermost function is an anonymous function inside another anonymous function, the context of the innermost function is different from the object that is hosting it. Therefore, `this` in this context is referencing the global context.

In order to preserve the context of `myOwnObject`, we can create a context in the first inner function and let the innermost function access this context. So we can rewrite our object definition as:

```
var name = "The window global";
var myOwnObject = {

  name: "My Own Object",

  getName: function(){
    var that = this;
    return function(){
      return that.name;
    };
  }
};

console.log(myOwnObject.getName()()); // displays "My Own Object"
```

Using this approach, we create a context inside the first inner function which references our object and then the innermost function can access this context, which is defined in its container (the first anonymous function). This results in the innermost anonymous function accessing the context of `myOwnObject` object.

As shown, it can be a little challenging to figure out what context `this` refers to at times but with practice and more experience you will become better at it. However, till then, don't take the context of `this` for granted and make sure that the context which you think `this` refers to is in fact the context that has been set for `this` in the code.

Closures

Now that we have had a brief discussion regarding execution context as it relates to `this`, it is time to talk about Closures. If you don't have a lot of experience with JavaScript, or if you are coming from more classical object oriented languages such as C++, you might find the concept of Closures a bit confusing in the beginning. In this section, I will try to take the mystery out of this concept and explain why Closures can be very useful in our code.

The main idea behind Closures is about preserving context and (mostly) how an inner function can keep the context of its containing parent.

Consider the following simple example:

```
function setTestValue(value){

  var firstNum = value || 2;

  return function(secondNum){
    if(firstNum > secondNum){
      return firstNum;
    }else if(firstNum < secondNum){
      return secondNum;
    }else{
      return "=";
    }
  };
}


var theNumberExaminer = setTestValue(6);
var result = theNumberExaminer(2);
console.log(result); // displays 6
```

As you can see, innermost function setTestValue takes a number as a parameter and sets it as the starting value to be used for comparison later.

When this function is executed, it also returns an anonymous function whose reference will be stored in the theNumberExaminer variable. This anonymous function is then used to compare a value passed to it with the value that was set as the starting value (firstNum) in the setTestValue function.

Note that we only pass one value (2) to theNumberExaminer to be compared against the starting number.

The question is: how does theNumberExaminer have access to the previous value passed to the setTestValue function?

Normally, when a function is returned, its execution context is removed and thus all the values related to that function's execution context are destroyed. However, with **Closures**, things work a little differently.

Here, the inner anonymous function is returned from the setTestValue function call (setTestValue(6)) and, with it, the execution context of its parent function. This allows the anonymous function to have access to the value of firstNum.

This relationship will hold as long as the inner function (the anonymous function) is not destroyed. The context of the parent object remains in memory because there is still a reference to the inner function.

The most important point is that Closures allow for inner functions to have access to the execution context of their parent functions (objects) as part of their scope chain. As values in the scope of the outer function change, the inner function can have access to the most recent values.

One advantage of creating and using Closures can be shown in the following example:

```
function myClosedObject (){
  var privateValue = 5;

  function privateFunc (){
    privateValue *= 2;
    return privateValue ;
  }

  // privileged method
  this.publicFunc = function(){

    return privateFunc();
  };
}

var firstObj = new myClosedObject ();
console.log(firstObj.publicFunc()); // displays 10
console.log(firstObj.publicFunc()); // displays 20
```

In the preceding code, we first create an instance of `myClosedObject` and then we execute the `publicFunc` of this instance. This call changes the value of `privateValue` from 5 to 10.

When we call this method one more time, the value of `privateValue` will change to 20. This is because after the first call to `publicFunc` the value of `privateValue` has been preserved (thanks to the created Closure). The second call to `publicFunc`, uses the most up to date value of `privateValue` (which is 10) to do its calculation, thus resulting in the value 20 being returned.

Encapsulation and scoping

As you may know, in JavaScript the idea of encapsulation is handled a little differently from most classical object oriented languages, since we really don't have a formal definition for classes (ECMAScript 6 introduces formal class definition).

When we create a variable inside a function using the keyword `var`, we are creating a **private** variable inside of that function, thus the scope of the variable is contained within the function. This also means that, if we use the function as a constructor function, such variables are not copied to the instances created using this constructor function.

Also, JavaScript does not have the concept of block scopes; instead it has function scope, so all the variables declared inside a function are accessible throughout the function block (ECMAScript 6 introduced block scopes).

Let's consider the following function declaration:

```
function simpleFunc () {
  var firstValue = 1;
  var secondValue = 2;
  this.instanceValue = 100;

  for(var i =0; i<50; i++){
    var thirdValue = firstValue + secondValue + i;
  }

  // displays "The final value of thirdValue is:52"
  console.log("The final value of thirdValue is:" + thirdValue);
}

simpleFunc();
```

As you can see, the `thirdValue` variable has been defined within the `for` loop block, but we can access it after the end of the `for` loop, since in JavaScript the scope of variables is bound to the scope of the container function and not the container block.

Of course, code external to this function cannot access such variables, as shown:

```
console.log(simpleFunc.firstValue); // displays undefined
```

As expected, the above code will produce `undefined` in the console.

We also cannot get access to `this.instanceValue` since inside a function `this` references the window object, as shown:

```
console.log(simpleFunc.instanceValue); // displays undefined
```

What happens if we use the preceding function as a constructor function and create an instance of the `simpleFunc` object?

Consider the following:

```
var testObj = new simpleFunc();
console.log(testObj.firstValue);    // displays undefined
console.log(testObj.instanceValue); // displays 100
```

As you know, when we define a variable with the `this` keyword, it is copied to the instances of the object and hence `testObj` has a copy of it and we can access it from the outside code.

However, if we take this a step further and create a private scope (**namespace**) inside the constructor function, then even the inner functions of the constructor function will not have access to it.

Consider the following:

```
function simpleFunc(){
  var firstValue = 1;
  (function(){
    var secondValue = 2;
    this.instanceValue = 100;
    console.log(firstValue); // shows 1

  })();

  //console.log(secondValue); //produces an error

}
```

The code above shows an immediately invoked anonymous function (also known as **IIFE**) inside our `simpleFunc` function, and even though this function has access to the execution context of its containing function, the containing function (`simpleFunc`) cannot access the variables and methods inside this inner function.

In fact, we have created a private namespace inside our `simpleFunc` that is completely hidden from the outside world.

The same is also true for when we create an instance of `simpleFunc` and try to access `this.inastanceValue`, since this variable is only accessible from inside the scope of the inner anonymous function.

This is shown here:

```
var testObj = new simpleFunc();
console.log(testObj.instanceValue); // displays undefined
```

As you can see, while JavaScript may not have the same form of encapsulation as classical object oriented languages, we can still create private scopes, and define variables and methods inside that scope that are not accessible from the outside code.

We will be re-visiting this concept and its usages a lot more when we design our application modules in future chapters.

You may also be asking yourself, "What if I want to create a constructor function which provides public methods, so I can access private members of the constructor function using these public methods?"

Let's consider the following constructor function:

```
function simpleFunc (){
  var privateValue = 1;
  this.readPrivateValue = function(){

    return privateValue;
  };
}

var testObj = new simpleFunc();
console.log(testObj.readPrivateValue());// displays 1
```

In this constructor, we have created a private member `privateValue` that is not accessible from the outside world. However, we have created a public method `this.readPrivateValue`, which can be accessed by the external code and can access the value of this private member.

So here, we have achieved two goals. First, we have kept our private member protected, and second, we have still provided read access to such private member through our public method.

The method `this.readPrivateValue` can be considered a **privileged method**, which means this public member has access to private members of the object.

Inheritance

If you have a background in classical object oriented languages such as C++, C#, or Java, you will be quite familiar with the concept of inheritance. In such languages, there are two types of inheritance: **interface inheritance** and **implementation inheritance**.

JavaScript however, only supports implementation inheritance, as there is no concept of function signature which is required for interface inheritance.

There are various ways of implanting inheritance in JavaScript and they all have their pros and cons. In this section, I will cover a few ways of implementing such relationship among objects and will briefly explain the advantages and disadvantages of each approach.

Prototype chaining

Let's start by creating two different constructor functions and an inheritance relationship between them.

Consider the following two function objects:

```
function BaseType (){
   this.baseValue = 2;
}

BaseType.prototype.getBaseValue = function(){
   return this.baseValue;
};

function ChildType (){
   this.childTypeValue = 50;
}
// creating inheritance relationship
ChildType.prototype = new BaseType();

ChildType.prototype.getChildTypeValue = function(){
   return this.childTypeValue;
};

var childInstance = new ChildType();

console.log(childInstance.getBaseValue()); // displays 2
console.log(childInstance.getChildTypeValue()); // displays 50
```

In the preceding code, we have created two extremely simple constructor functions. As you can see, we have defined a simple property for each one of them which are methods related to each object. However, we have created these simple methods as properties of the `prototype` object for each function as opposed to directly creating them on the constructor functions.

If you are familiar with the `prototype` property, you know that every function has this property by default. The value of this property is an object that is shared with all the instances that are created using the constructor function.

The advantage of creating methods (properties) on `prototype` object as opposed to on the constructor function itself is that by doing so, all the instances that are created using the constructor share these methods. Therefore, these instances do not have to have their own copy of these properties, thus optimizing our code's performance and memory usage.

In the preceding code, in the case of `BaseType`, we simply augmented the `prototype` object of this constructor with a method called `getBaseValue`, but for `ChildType`, we did something a little different.

We first created an instance of `BaseType` and then we assigned it to `ChildType` using the following expression:

```
ChildType.prototype = new BaseType();
```

After the above assignment, the `ChildType.prototype` value becomes an instance of `BaseType`. This means that this `prototype` object has access to two properties now, `baseValue` and `getBaseValue`.

The end result is that there are two properties that instances of `ChildType` have access to but didn't need to create them.

When we run the following line of code:

```
console.log(childInstance.getBaseValue()); //displays 2
```

The `childInstance` variable can return the value of the `baseValue` variable, using `getBaseValue` method.

Of course, `childInstance` also has access to its own variable `childTypeValue`. If we run the following code, `50` will be displayed.

```
console.log(childInstance.getChildTypeValue()); // displays 50
```

Property look up in prototype chaining

Let's examine how `ChildInstance` gets access to the properties of `BaseType` in a little more depth.

When we try to access a property on `ChildInstance`, behind the scenes, a search is conducted on the instance itself to see if that property is available. If the property is not found, then the search continues to the `prototype` object of the `ChildInstance` object. Since an instance of `BaseType` is the value of the `prototype` object belonging to `ChildInstance`, the search is continued in `BaseType`.

But there is more, the instance of BaseType (which is the value of the prototype object belonging to ChildType) itself has a prototype object and our ChildType prototype has a link to this prototype object. That prototype object has a property called getBaseValue. Since this method has access to the BaseType properties, it can return the value of baseValue.

You can think of how this lookup is conducted as shown here:

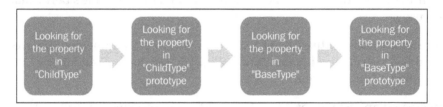

As you can see, there is quite a bit of searching taking place in order to find the instance property. Also, keep in mind that if the property was not found in the prototype of BaseType, the search would have continued to the prototype object of the parent of all objects in JavaScript, the Object type. Let's talk about how that works.

Remember that every function has a prototype property which its value is an object. This prototype object itself has a prototype property which its value is the prototype object of the Object type.

That is why, when we call the BaseType.toString method, even though we have not defined this method on BaseType or its prototype object, the call still succeeds and produces the string value of the object. The toString method is defined on the prototype object of Object type, and thus is available to all the children of Object type.

It is very important to keep in mind that the search is ceased and will not continue any further in the chain of protoypes, as soon as the property that the search is being conducted for is found.

To make it a little more clear, let's modify our ChildType to have a property (method) called getBaseValue. Doing so will result in what is known as **shadowing** (or masking) of this property on BaseType.

So, if we modify the code for ChildType as below:

```
function ChildType (){
  this.childTypeValue = 50;
}
// creating inheritance relationship
```

```
ChildType.prototype = new BaseType();

ChildType.prototype.getChildTypeValue = function(){
  return this.childTypeValue;
};
ChildType.prototype.getBaseValue = function(){
  return this.childTypeValue;
};
var childInstance = new ChildType();
console.log(childInstance.getBaseValue()); // displays 50
```

The call to `childInstance.getBaseValue` will now return the value 50 instead of 2. This is because as soon as the search for the `getBaseValue` method (property) finds this method on `ChildType`, it will not search any further and will execute this method. This of course, will return the value of the `childTypeValue` property.

One other thing that we need to keep in mind, is the fact that because of the relationship that has been created among all these reference types, the following instance check will return `true` for all of them.

```
console.log(childInstance instanceof Object);    // displays true
console.log(childInstance instanceof BaseType);  // displays true
console.log(childInstance instanceof ChildType); // displays true
```

You can use this test to see if one reference type is inheriting properties from another reference type.

While prototype chaining has many advantages and allows us to create inheritance among our base objects and our child objects, it has the disadvantage that any changes to the base object's reference type properties are reflected in all the instances of the child classes. This at times may not be a desirable effect and you need to be aware of it.

Resetting the constructor property

Every `prototype` object has a `constructor` property. This property always refers back to the constructor function itself. When we overwrite the `prototype` property completely as we did in the previous code by setting it like so:

```
ChildType.prototype = new BaseType();
```

The `constructor` property of the `prototype` object will be referencing the parent object. This can be examined as below:

```
console.log(childInstance.constructor);
```

Which displays:

```
function BaseType(){
   this.baseValue = 2;
}
```

It is always a good idea to reset the `constructor` property of the `prototype` object after it has been completely replaced, as follows:

```
ChildType.prototype.constructor = ChildType;
```

This is so the `prototype` object can correctly point back to the correct constructor object.

The reset enables us to correctly find the constructor object of the instance as shown:

```
console.log(childInstance.constructor);
```

Which now correctly reports the following:

```
function ChildType(){
   this.childTypeValue = 50;
}
```

We will discuss the `constructor` property some more, later in this chapter.

Constructor stealing

Another approach to creating inheritance in JavaScript is using a technique known as **constructor stealing,** which is similar to classical inheritance in other object oriented languages.

Consider the following:

```
function BaseType(){
   this.baseValue = 2;
}
function ChildType(){
   BaseType.call(this);
}
ChildType.prototype.getBaseTypeValue = function(){
   return this.baseValue;
};
var instanceObj = new ChildType();

console.log(instanceObj.getBaseTypeValue());   // displays 2
```

In the above code, we are using the `call` method to execute `BaseType` in the context of `ChildType`. This results in `ChildType` instances getting a copy of all the properties of `BaseType`. Since each instance of `ChildType` now has its own copy of the properties, modifying the properties of `BaseType` is not reflected in the child instances.

This approach, however, has its own issues. The main issue is that since we are not assigning an instance of `BaseType` to the `prototype` object of `ChildType`, the properties defined on the `prototype` object of `BaseType` are not shared among the instances of `ChildType`. This will no result in the most efficient approach in implementing inheritance and does not allow for code sharing of the parent's `prototype` object properties among child instances.

Parasitic combination inheritance

Another way to create inheritance relationships among reference types is to use a combination of the techniques that we have already discussed, while eliminating their inefficiencies. This is also my favorite technique for creating inheritance.

Let's modify the code that we have already seen, so we can implement this approach:

```
function BaseType () {

  this.baseValue = 2;
  this.secondBaseValue = 99;
}

BaseType.prototype.getBaseValue = function(){
  return this.baseValue;
};

function ChildType () {
  BaseType.call(this);
  this.childTypeValue = 50;
}

// creating inheritance relationship
ChildType.prototype = BaseType.prototype;

ChildType.prototype.getChildTypeValue = function(){
  return this.childTypeValue;
};
```

```
var childInstance1 = new ChildType();
var childInstance2 = new ChildType();
childInstance1.baseValue = 100;
childInstance2.baseValue = 55;

console.log(childInstance1.getBaseValue()); //displays 100
console.log(childInstance1.getChildTypeValue()); //displays 50
console.log(childInstance1.secondBaseValue); //displays 99

console.log(childInstance2.getBaseValue()); //displays 55
console.log(childInstance2.getChildTypeValue()); //displays 50
console.log(childInstance2.secondBaseValue); // displays 99
```

In this latest implementation, we are using the `call` method in the `ChildType` constructor to copy all the properties of `BaseType`. This provides the child object instance with the ability to modify the properties of `BaseType`, which only affects that particular instance of `ChildType` and does not get reflected in other instances of `ChildType`.

In our example, this type of inheritance is initiated in the following statement in the `ChildType` constructor:

```
BaseType.call(this);
```

We also have assigned the `prototype` of `BaseType` to `ChildType`, as shown:

```
ChildType.prototype = BaseType.prototype;
```

Note that we have assigned only the `prototype` object of `BaseType` to the `prototype` object of `ChildType`, thus eliminating the second call to the `BaseType` constructor, resulting in more efficient code.

This approach also has the advantage of allowing us to share all the properties that have been defined on the `prototype` object of `BaseType` among all the instances of the child object. Therefore, not every child object instance will have its own copy of such properties, which in turn leads to better code efficiency and memory management.

Once we create an instance of `ChildType`, this instance has access to copied properties from `BaseType` as well as all the shared properties defined on the `prototype` object of `BaseType`. Of course, each instance also has access to all of its own properties defined on the `ChildType` constructor and on the `ChildType` prototype object.

Parasitic combination inheritance provides us with the best of both previously discussed techniques (**prototype chaining** and **constructor stealing**) and it is widely used by many experienced JavaScript developers.

Constructor property

Every object in JavaScript has a `constructor` property that references the constructor object that was used to create the instance of that object.

For instance, in all functions, the `constructor` property has a reference to the `Function` type constructor. We could verify this by executing the following statement:

```
console.log(ChildType.constructor); // references
    Function type constructor
```

Since `prototype` property's value is an object too, it also has a `constructor` property. However, this `constructor` property references the object (function) itself. So if we examine this property **before** we assign the `BaseType.prototype` object to `ChildType.prototype`, as follows:

```
console.log(ChildType.prototype.constructor); //
    references ChildType
```

We can see that this property is referencing the object that `prototype` belongs to, which in this case is `ChildType`.

As mentioned previously, if we completely replace the `prototype` object , as in the case of the following statement, which was used in implementing our previous inheritance:

```
ChildType.prototype = BaseType.prototype;
```

We overwrite the value of the `constructor` property on the `prototype` object of `Childtype`.

If we examine the `constructor` property of the `prototype` object now, it will be referencing `BaseType`, instead of `Childtype`.

```
console.log(ChildType.prototype.constructor) //
    references BaseType
```

As seen before, we need to reset the `constructor` property of the `prototype` object as shown:

```
ChildType.prototype.constructor = ChildType;
```

Keep in mind that resetting the `constructor` property needs to happen after the `prototype` object has been re-written and not before. Otherwise, the re-write will completely remove the `constructor` property.

The following is an example of how this should be done:

```
ChildType.prototype = BaseType.prototype;
ChildType.prototype.constructor = ChildType;
```

I encourage you to examine all the code discussed in this section closely to understand how all the pieces are tied together and how inheritance works among objects.

Native support for inheritance

Now that we have had a look at different techniques for creating inheritance among constructor functions, it is a good idea to consider native support for creating such relationships in JavaScript.

ECMAScript 5 provides **prototypal inheritance** by way of `Object.create()` method.

This method accepts two parameters. The first parameter is the object to be used as the `prototype` (base object) for the new object. The second parameter is optional and is used to add additional properties to the new object.

Consider the following code:

```
var BaseType = {
    firstValue: 20,
    secondValue: [3,4]
};
var ChildType1 = Object.create(BaseType);

ChildType1.secondValue.push(5);

ChildType1.getBaseTypeFirstValue = function(){
    return this.firstValue ;
};

var ChildType2 = Object.create(BaseType);
ChildType2.newProperty = 50;

console.log(ChildType1.getBaseTypeFirstValue()); // displays 20
console.log(ChildType1.secondValue); // displays [3, 4, 5]

console.log(ChildType2.secondValue); // displays [3, 4, 5]
console.log(BaseType.secondValue); // displays [3, 4, 5]
```

There are some interesting points that you need to keep in mind regarding the preceding code. As you can see, we have used the `BaseType` constructor and have passed it to the `Object.create` method to create an instance of our `BaseType` object and assign it to the `ChildType1` variable.

We then have added a new value to the property `secondValue` array of this new object (`ChildType1`). In the next line, we have also added a new method, `getBaseTypeFirstValue` to this instance.

When we create a second object `ChildType2` using the method `Object.create`, and examine the value of the `secondValue` array, we see that the value is as shown below:

```
console.log(ChildType2.secondValue); // displays [3, 4, 5]
```

This is because the modified property `secondValue` is shared among all the instances that have inheritance relationships with the base object `BaseType`. Thus, all the changes done to the properties of the base object by one child instance are reflected in all the instances, as well as in the base object, `BaseType` itself. This is shown here:

```
console.log(BaseType.secondValue); // displays [3, 4, 5]
```

This is an important point to keep in mind.

As previously mentioned, we could also use the second optional parameter of the `Object.create` method to add new properties to the child instance at the same time that we create the inheritance relationship between the base and the child object.

Consider the following:

```
var BaseType = {
  firstValue: 20,
  secondValue: [3,4]
};
var ChildType = Object.create(BaseType, {
  optionalObject:{
    value: 50
  }
});

console.log(ChildType.optionalObject); // displays 50
console.log(ChildType.firstValue); // displays 20
```

The `ChildType` object has now inherited all the properties of the `BaseType` object and has a new property `optionalObject`, which is specific to this instance of the child object.

Even though this is a native way for creating inheritance among objects in ECMAScript 5, I have found this technique to not be as popular as parasitic combination inheritance.

I personally find this approach to be a little too verbose in comparison to the other approaches that we covered in this chapter for implementing inheritance but it allows us to define attributes of the new property exactly as we like.

 You can refer to the following online resource for more information regarding the Object.create method:

https://developer.mozilla.org/en-US/docs/Web/
JavaScript/Reference/Global_Objects/Object/create

Summary

The goal of this chapter was to provide a quick overview of some OOP concepts in JavaScript. Having a good understanding of these concepts is important as we will be using them in implementing our modular architecture in the following chapters.

In this chapter, we looked at various ways of creating objects as well as concepts such as closure, encapsulation, and inheritance.

The assumption that I made was that you likely have a fairly good experience with JavaScript and are probably familiar with at least some of these concepts.

My intent was to provide "just enough" of a review of JavaScript OOP concepts to get you ready for future chapters.

There are many good resources available that can help you extend your knowledge of Object Oriented JavaScript principles further.

Two of my personal favorites on this topic are:

- *Object-Oriented JavaScript, Stoyan Stefanov, Kumar Chetan Sharma*
- *Professional JavaScript for Web Developers, Nicholas C. Zakas*

In the next chapter, we will start focusing on a popular design pattern known as **Module Design Pattern** to get us ready for creating simple modules in our application.

3

Module Design Pattern

Now that we have reviewed some important JavaScript OOP concepts in the previous chapter, we are going to leverage some of the techniques discussed to create modules and start using them in our application.

You are probably familiar with the term **design pattern**, which is essentially a way of structuring code as a reusable solution for common programming problems. In this chapter, we are going to focus on a particular design pattern in JavaScript called **module pattern**.

We will explore how we can create simple modules using this pattern and then we will build upon these modules to create our application's modules in the following chapters.

Module pattern is one of the most frequently used patterns in JavaScript for creating modular applications.

Some of the topics that we will discuss in this chapter are:

- Structure of module pattern
- Internal private scope in module pattern
- How to create simple modules
- How to create a module factory

Module pattern

In the previous chapter, we had a look at how we can create private variables and namespaces inside functions. We also explored how private scopes can be implemented. Some concepts related to private scopes can also be applied to **singleton** objects residing inside functions.

A singleton object is an object there will only ever be one instance of it in the application. Singleton objects can be created using object literal notation, which we saw examples of in the previous chapter.

Consider the following object definition:

```
var mySingletonObj = {};
```

While the preceding object does not do anything, it is in fact a valid object and there can only be one instance of this object as we cannot create other objects based on mySingletonObj.

Let's add some value properties and methods (method properties) to this object and see how we can access such properties outside of the object definition:

```
var mySingletonObj = {

  name: "Sasan",

  title: "Software Developer",

  getName: function(){

    return this.name;
  },

  getTitle: function(){

    return this.title;
  }

};
// displays "Sasan"
console.log(mySingletonObj.getName());

// displays "Software Developer"
console.log(mySingletonObj.getTitle());
```

In the above object definition, we have created a singleton object with four properties. Two of them are value properties and two are method properties.

Our method properties have access to our value properties and return their values. However, we can also directly access the object's properties and even override their values from outside of the object.

Have a look at the following code snippet:

```
mySingletonObj.name = "John";
console.log(mySingletonObj.name); // displays "John"
```

This shows that, while we have encapsulation (I am using the term loosely here) in our code, we do not have access control and the external code can change the values of the properties in our object. This at times, is undesirable.

Let's re-factor our code and create a simple module, using the module pattern. This will help us implement encapsulations as well as access control in our singleton object.

Consider the following:

```
var mySingletonObj = (function(){

    //private variables
    var name = "Sasan";
    var title = "Software Developer";

    //returning a Singleton
    return {

        // privileged method
        getName : function(){

            return name;
        },
        // privileged method
        getTitle: function(){

            return title;
        }

    };

})();
```

In the preceding code, we have created an **Immediately Invoked Function Expression (IIFE)** and have assigned its return value (which is a singleton object) to the variable mySingletonObj.

The returned singleton object has two methods that have access to the private variables of the container function and return their related values.

If we try to access the function variables directory from the returned object such as:

```
console.log(mySingletonObj.name); // displays undefined
```

We are unable to do so. This is because the `name` property is a private property of the container function and it does not exist on the returned anonymous object.

However, we can access this property through the privileged method `getName`, which is defined on the singleton object returned by our IIFE.

As the `mySingletonObj` variable has a reference to this singleton object, if we execute the following code:

```
console.log(mySingletonObj.getName()); // displays "Sasan"
```

We are able to access the value assigned to the `name` property of the function. Note that the singleton object returned from the IIFE still has access to the context of the anonymous function that contains it. This is possible because we have created a closure here. Of course, the same applies to the `title` property of the function as seen here:

```
// displays "Software Developer"
console.log(mySingletonObj.getTitle());
```

This approach of structuring our code in such a way that a returned singleton object from inside a function provides access to the private members (internal private scope) of the container function object) is what forms the basis of module pattern in JavaScript.

Internal private scope in module pattern

Module pattern enables us to create a private scope for our code inside a function while providing controlled access to such a private scope through an interface. This interface can be in the form of a returned singleton object.

In the code example in the previous section, `mySingletonObj` is the interface to the private scope of our IIFE.

What happens if we add another property to `mySingletonObj` that has the same identifier as one of the properties of the containing function?

Well, `mySingletonObj` is like any other object in the sense that we can add properties to it regardless of it containing the object's properties. However, the important thing to remember here is that assigning or modifying such properties on the returned interface has no effect on the private variables encapsulated in the function that contains the returned object.

Let's modify our previous module and dig a little deeper:

```
var mySingletonObj = function() {
    //private variables
    var name = "Sasan";
    var title = "Software Developer";

    //returning a singleton
    return {
        name: 'Tom',

        // privileged method
        getOuterName: function() {
            return name;
        },

        // privileged method
        getInnerName: function() {
            return this.name;
        },

        // privileged method
        getTitle: function() {
            return title;
        }
    };
}();
```

As you can see, we have added a name property to our returned singleton object from the IIFE, which has the same identifier as the name property on the function object. We have also replaced one of the previous methods with two new methods in our interface (the singleton object returned from the IIFE). The first method, getOuterName, simply returns the value of the name property.

The question is, which name property, the one from the private scope of the function or the name property from the singleton object itself?

If we run the following line of code:

```
console.log(mySingletonObj.name); // displays "Tom"
```

We can see that the value returned is the value in the scope of the singleton object itself; thus, Tom is displayed.

However, if we try to access the same property, using the method property on the interface, a different value will be returned. Have a look at the following code snippet:

```
console.log(mySingletonObj.getOuterName()); // displays "Sasan"
```

As you can see, the value returned from this method is the value for the `name` property from the outer scope of the interface, which is the scope of the container function. This can be rather confusing.

If the intent is to return the value for the name property which is defined inside the singleton object itself (the interface), we need to qualify the property using the `this` keyword.

Have a look at the second new method that we added to our module:

```
getInnerName: function(){

    return this.name;
}
```

In this method, we specifically qualify the context for `name` using the `this` keyword, which references the context of the singleton object itself as opposed to the containing function. Thus, if we run the following code:

```
console.log(mySingletonObj.getInnerName()); // displays "Tom"
```

The value assigned to `name` in the context of the singleton object is returned. This is an important distinction to keep in mind.

Adding properties to an interface in module pattern

Now that we have seen how internal private scope is at in play when we use the module pattern, let's see what happens if we add new dynamic properties to the singleton object returned in our previous example.

Consider the following line of code:

```
mySingletonObj.name = "Jack";
```

Here, we are simply adding a new property dynamically to our object `mySingletonObj`. This property happens to have the same identifier as an already existing property on the object. What happens to the original value of the `name` property?

We can find out by running the following tests:

```
console.log(mySingletonObj.name); // displays "Jack"
console.log(mySingletonObj.getOuterName()); // displays "Sasan"
console.log(mySingletonObj.getInnerName()); // displays "Jack"
```

As you can see, the new value of the singleton object's property is displayed regardless of whether we directly access the property or use our singleton's method to return the value of the property.

On the other hand, as expected, no changes have taken place in the value of the property contained in the container function's context, even though our singleton object does have access to this context.

Remember, when we use the module pattern in JavaScript and return a singleton object from it (as an interface to the containing object/function), there are two contexts that are at play.

First, the internal private scope of the container function, which our singleton object has access to through closure.

The second is the context of the singleton object itself as with any other object in JavaScript. It is important to understand the distinction between the two contexts when you design your modules using the module pattern in JavaScript.

Another important point to keep in mind is that the code structure (pattern) shown previously allows us to have both object encapsulation and access control on the properties defined in a private namespace. In this case, the anonymous function creates a namespace that returns an anonymous object or, more accurately, a reference to the anonymous object (the singleton object) as an interface.

This approach becomes very valuable since now we can be sure that no external code is able to either intentionally or accidentally change the values of the properties in our namespace. This structure provides control over what properties are accessible by the outside code and what properties are hidden away and protected in the private scope.

Object factory module

We can design our modules to be very specialized chunks of code that do very specific tasks, while protecting their internals from external code interferences. So far, we have looked at a very simple pattern for creating modules. We can take this pattern a step further and design a module that creates instances of an object, adds properties to these instances, and then returns them to the code external to the module.

Consider the following module:

```javascript
var myCarFactoryModule = function() {

    var createdCars = [];

    function carFactory() {
        // could also use "var newCar = {}";
        var newCar = new Object();

        newCar.type = arguments[0];
        newCar.color = arguments[1];
        newCar.gearType = arguments[2];
        newCar.cylinder = arguments[3];
        createdCars.push(newCar);
        return newCar;
    }
    return {

        // privileged method
        createCar: function(type, color, gearType, cylinder) {
            return carFactory(type, color, gearType, cylinder);
        },

        // privileged method
        getCarCount: function() {
            return createdCars.length;
        },

        // privileged method
        removeCar: function(index) {
            createdCars.splice(index, 1);
        }
    };
}();
```

As you can see in this code, we have combined two patterns together: the **object factory** pattern and the module pattern.

Design patterns in JavaScript

If you are not familiar with design patterns in general or would like to become more familiar with design patterns in JavaScript, I highly recommend the following resource:

Mastering JavaScript Design Patterns by *Simon Timms.*

When our function `myCarFactoryModule` is called, based on the parameters passed in, we create an instance of a car and then we assign it to an array which is the repository for all instances of the cars created. We have designed this module in such a way that the external code to the module has no access to the method that creates the cars, nor has access to the car repository.

Let's test this using the following code:

```
var myFirstCar = myCarFactoryModule.createCar("Sedan",
  "red", "automatic",4); // creates first instance of car

var mySecondCar = myCarFactoryModule.createCar("SUV",
  "Silver", "Standard",6); // creates second instance of car

console.log(myFirstCar.color); // displays "red"
console.log(mySecondCar.gearType); // displays "Standard"

var myTotalCars = myCarFactoryModule.getCarCount();
console.log(myTotalCars); //displays 2

myCarFactoryModule.removeCar(0); // removes the first care object

var myTotalCars = myCarFactoryModule.getCarCount();
console.log(myTotalCars); // displays 1
```

As you can see, the outside code can call our module's interface to create cars and also get a count on the number of the cars created. It can also remove a car, if it is desired to do so.

There are three privileged methods in this module: `createCar`, `getCarCount`, and `removeCar`. You can think of these methods as bridges between the internals of the module, which are hidden away from the outside world, and the external code, which relies on the internals of the module to do some specific tasks.

The privileged methods (which are members of the singleton interface object) are exposed to the external code to provide the module's functionality to whoever needs its services.

There is a notable advantage to this design. As you might have noticed, we can modify the code inside our module and add additional functionality to the module without affecting how other parts of our application can interact with our module.

This is true, as long as we don't change the name or the functionality of the privileged methods that provide access for the external code to utilize the module's functionality.

At the same time, we can add new privileged methods to the interface of the module or modify the internals of our current privileged methods in the singleton object without affecting the internal code of the module itself.

This allows us to have a good separation of concerns and responsibilities between the exposed part of our module (the module's interface) and the private internals of the module.

Creating loose coupling among modules

In a modular design, an application is often created using many modules. In order for these modules to work together, we need to create coupling among them, without the modules being tightly dependent on each other.

Let's create an application based on a few simple modules and have the modules interact with each other in a loosely coupled manner. Of course, we will keep this application very simple for now. In later chapters, we will take the concepts utilized in this application and build upon them to create our fully modularized application ecosystem.

I'm making the safe assumption here that our future application will consist of many separate modules, with each one of them being responsible for doing a very specific task.

We will start by creating our core application module and calling it `ApplicationInitModule`. Usually, the very first step in running an application is to take care of the application's initialization tasks. Our `ApplicationInitModule` will be designed to do just that.

In the following code snippet, when `ApplicationInitModule` is started, it will in turn start all the registered modules and their initialization routines. This process will take care of the application's initialization routine as a whole.

Have a look at the following code and see how our application is designed:

```
var ApplicationInitModule = function() {
    var registeredModules = [];

    return {
        registerModule: function(module) {
            registeredModules.push(module);
        },
        getAppModulesCount: function() {
            return registeredModules.length;
        },
        removeRegisteredModule: function(index) {
            registeredModules.splice(index, 1);
        },
        initializeAllModules: function() {
            for (var module in registeredModules) {
                registeredModules[module].initialize();
            }
        },
    };
}();

var GlobalApp = (function() {
    var registerModule = ApplicationInitModule.registerModule;
    return {
        registerModule: registerModule
    };
})();

var testModule1 = (function() {
    var self = {};
    var moduleName = "Module 1";

    self.initialize = function() {
        //displays "testmodule1 has been initialized!"
        console.log("testmodule1 has been initialized!");
        //displays "module name is: Module 1"
        console.log("module name is: " + moduleName);
    };

    (function() {
        GlobalApp.registerModule(self);
    })();

    return {
        initialize: self.initialize,
```

```
        getName: function() {
            return moduleName;
        }
    };
}) ();

var testModule2 = (function() {
    var moduleName = "Module 2";

    function initialize() {
        //displays "testmodule2 has been initialized!"
        console.log("testmodule2 has been initialized!");
    }
    return {
        initialize: initialize
    };
}) ();
GlobalApp.registerModule(testModule2);
```

As you can see, a few interesting things are taking place in this application, but all the techniques used, we have already discussed in this book. Nonetheless, I'll go through each piece and explain the inner workings of each module.

Application core module

The code starts by defining `ApplicationInitModule` as an application initializer module. The purpose of this module is to register all the available modules in the application (store them in an array) and then initialize them all (one at a time), when the application runs.

This module also provides an interface with some hooks for the external code to interact with it. As you can see, there are methods to register a module, get the count of all the modules registered in the app for initialization, and remove a module from the list of registered modules; of course, there is also a method to initialize all modules that have been registered with the app.

In this module, we are using an IIFE to return a reference to an anonymous singleton object, which is essentially the interface of the module.

One of the points that I'd like to draw your attention to is the fact that the functionality of this module is really defined in its interface. However, the module didn't have to be designed in this manner. You can also see that, in the other modules shown in the previous code, I have not used this approach. This is so you can see how we can implement the module pattern in various ways.

Application Mediator module

Our `GlobalApp` module also uses an IIFE to return a singleton object as the interface to the module. The whole purpose of this module is to act as a mediator (abstraction layer) between `testModule1`, `testModule2`, and our core module, `ApplicationInitModule`.

We have designed the application this way so we can create a loose coupling between our core module and the other registered modules. As you can see, `GlobalApp` has been designed as a very thin layer.

This thin layer allows us to change our core module (`ApplicationInitModule`) as we please and even change its interface to the outside world, without affecting the other modules that rely on this module's functionality.

In our design, the only module which relies directly on the `ApplicationInitModule` interface is our `GlobalApp` module. This means that, if there are any changes to the interface of `ApplicationInitModule`, we only need to make modifications to our thin mediator layer `GlobalApp`. All the other modules in the application will be unaffected, as they still use the same thin layer interface provided by `GlobalApp`.

You will see in the future chapters of this book that this thin layer is called the **sandbox** and we will be using this concept of sandboxing to isolate our application modules/components from our application's core module(s). We will also use the same technique to isolate the modules/components from each other. For now, just try to become familiar with the general idea of module isolation (sandboxing) as shown in the previous application.

Application non-core modules

In our application implementation, we have created two simple modules that register themselves with the core module and really do nothing other than announcing to the world that they have been initialized.

Let's have a closer look at how these modules have been implemented.

testModule1 implementation

In `testModule1`, we have created an empty object called `self`, which gets augmented with a method called `initialize`. This is the method that will be called when our core module tries to initialize this module.

The registration of this module with the core module happens using an internal IIFE, which in turn calls our mediator module GlobalApp with a reference to the object self. This is implemented as shown below:

```
(function(){

    GlobalApp.registerModule(self);

})();
```

Of course, the GlobalApp.registerModule method is in fact a reference to the core module's method, ApplicationInitModule.registerModule. However, testModule1 does not know that and is only aware of GlobalApp provided interface, GlobalApp.registerModule.

We have also used an IIFE to return an interface to this module, which is available through the testModule1 variable.

Note that the interface provides two properties. One is a reference to the self.initialize method of the module and the other, getName, simply returns the value of the encapsulated and hidden moduleName variable. Also note that moduleName is not a property on the self object. Instead, it is implemented as a containing function's property.

testModule2 implementation

Our testModule2 is implemented a little differently in comparison to testModule1. As shown in the code, we have simply defined a function inside our module called initialize that is exposed to the external code indirectly through the interface returned from our IIFE for this module.

In our testModule2, the moduleName variable is completely sealed from the outside world as there are no methods defined on the interface to provide access to this variable.

There is also no internal IIFE that registers the module with our core module, ApplicationInitModule, thus we need to make a call outside of our module definition to achieve this task, as shown here:

```
GlobalApp.registerModule(testModule2);
```

Notice that we have used our mediator module GlobalApp for this registration again and we are not directly calling the related method on the core module. This allows us to still preserve our loose coupling among the modules.

Design Pattern used in testModule2

The way we have implemented `testModule2` is based on a design pattern known as **revealing module pattern**, in its simplest form. This is a very popular pattern for designing modules but of course there are various ways of implementing modules, as we have already seen. We will see even more patterns for implementing modules in the upcoming chapters. To get a better understanding of this pattern, please refer to previously mentioned resource for JavaScript design patterns.

Auto-initialization of application modules

So far we have seen how our application modules use a mediator module to register themselves with our application's core module, without being aware of the existence of the core module.

We also noted that communication among modules was done through the interfaces that were provided by the modules to the outside world. Only such interfaces had access to the internals of the modules and their internal private scope.

The following diagram depicts the relationships that exist among our application modules and provides an overall view of our application:

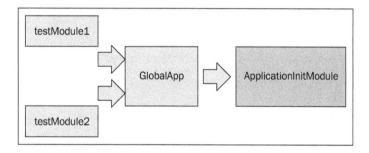

Let's have a look at the method in the core module that is responsible for calling initialization methods on all of our registered modules.

Remember that a reference to each application module registered with the core module has been added to the array `registeredModules`. This is shown in the following code snippet:

```
registerModule : function(module){

        registeredModules.push(module);
}
```

When we call the `initializeAllModules` method in our application (on the core module), a `for` loop is used to call the `initialize` method on all the registered modules. This is done as follows:

```
initializeAllModules: function(){

    for(var module in registeredModules){

        registeredModules[module].initialize();

    }
};
```

As you can see, `initializeAllModules` has no idea what each registered module's `initialize` method does when it is called. All it knows is to call the `initialize` method on the registered module and let the module take care of its own initialization tasks.

This is a very important point when we modularize our code. Each module only deals with tasks that are specific to that module's design and none of the other modules have any knowledge of how such tasks are done in that module.

This means, while our core module calls the `initialize` method on one or many modules, it does not directly get involved with the initialization tasks of each module.

It is time to run a test and see how application initialization takes place. Consider the following:

```
// displays
// "testmodule1 has been initialized!"
// "module name is: Module 1"
// "testmodule2 has been initialized!"
ApplicationInitModule.initializeAllModules();
```

When we run the preceding code, we can see that both of our modules report that they have been successfully initialized.

Of course, we have designed our application in such a way that all the registered modules do have an accessible method called `initialize`. This allows us to use an array and a `for` loop to initialize them all in sequence.

Module initialization and design considerations

At the application design time, you decide on how the modules should be initialized and how the initialization method in each module should be called. The important point is that calling the initialization routine of each module should not cause a tight coupling.

For consistency reasons, as well as ease of maintainability, I usually name the methods which are responsible for initialization tasks in all of my application modules: `initialize` or `init`. This allows me to use a `for` loop to call all the registered modules in sequence and ask the modules to initialize themselves accordingly.

Keep in mind that creating loose coupling among modules is only possible as long as the interfaces (public method hooks) in our modules do not change their names and their accessibility for the external code.

This means that, for example, if `testModule1` calls the `GlobalApp.registerModule` method to register itself, it should always be able to call that method for registration. This should hold true even if the mechanism of how this registration takes place changes internally in the `GlobalApp` object.

The architecture and design that you saw in our simple application here creates a foundation for creating loose coupling among our application modules. This in turn leads to a more extensible and maintainable implementation for both small and large applications.

You can look at module interfaces as contracts among modules, which enables them to interact with each other regardless of how the internals of such contracts are implemented. Note that, while there are contracts among modules in the application, there is no direct dependency among them. Each module is free to decide on how to implement its specific functionality to accomplish the tasks that it was designed to do.

This is so, as long as the module provides the functionality and the service which is expected from it.

This approach will provide a great deal of flexibility and extensibility for our application. It allows us to add, remove, and modify various parts of our application in a very targeted and manageable manner without such changes having an impact on other pieces of the application.

The fundamental architectural concepts that we discussed here are the concepts that will form the building blocks of the final application that we will build in this book.

Summary

In this chapter, we looked at one of the most popular design patterns in JavaScript: module pattern.

By creating simple modules, we explored various aspects of internal private scope in module pattern and saw how modules can interact with each other, without having access to the protected properties of each other's private scope.

This pattern allows us to create encapsulation and access control in our objects and modules, while providing an interface for the external code to leverage the implemented functionality intended for external use.

One of the most important aspect of module pattern is how it can be used to create a modular design for our application as a whole. This enables us to create loose coupling among our modules, which are essentially the building blocks of our application.

In later chapters, we will utilize this approach and slowly build more complex modules to create a robust and easily maintainable code base for our application. These modules can also be easily reused as needed, in all of our future applications.

4
Designing Simple Modules

In this chapter, we are going to focus on applying the concepts that we have learned in the previous chapters to design some simple modules for our application.

We will start by analyzing our application's functionality as a whole and then we will break it down into smaller functional pieces. Once we have decided on our application's functional pieces, we will start creating simple modules to implement the required functionality.

This chapter is meant to demonstrate the possible steps in the beginning of our application's life cycle, based on our requirements. The goal is to see how using modules can help us design a better architecture and get a feel for the practical advantages of a modular design.

The simple modules that we create in this chapter will provide the foundation for our final application in this book, which will be a working client-side single page application.

In this chapter we will cover:

- Reflecting the overall application requirements in our design
- Designing the application's main pieces
- Creating specialized modules for our application's main pieces
- Collaboration among modules
- Using object definitions to describe page fragments
- Dynamically generating pages and page fragments

The big picture

Before we start any coding at all, we need to have a good understanding of what our application is all about, what the requirements are, and what possible functional pieces are needed to satisfy our requirements.

While in the beginning of an application's design phase, we try to answer as many questions as possible regarding our application's requirements, we should always try not to get too tied down by the details.

The idea is to get the big picture right, understand what it is that we want to deliver, the timelines involved, and the resources available. Based on such analyses, we can start creating a scalable, flexible, and extensible architectural design for our application.

I'd like to draw your attention to a very important word that I used here, **extensible**. The ability of an application to be easily extended is very important in a proper design. Keep in mind that no matter how much we try to finalize all of the requirements for an application ahead of time, we won't be able to foresee them all in the beginning.

Requirements change over time, new requirements are added, and old requirements get modified or even removed altogether from the final draft of the application. The key is to design our application in a way that can accommodate all such changes without a big impact on the overall architecture. This is where the advantages of a modular architecture shine and help to mitigate the adverse effects that such changes might have on the application as a whole.

As we keep these points in mind, let's talk about the application that we are going to build together in this book.

Our application requirements

Our application is a simple yet fully functional image gallery application. The goal is to present the users with a catalog of beautiful images on our site. Our site visitors can click each of the images to see a full view of the image and add the images to their favorite list of images, if they wish to do so.

The application will have a header, a navigation bar at the top, a main content area in the middle, a footer, and of course a logo.

As you can tell, there are not many complicated pieces at play here, but I assure you that under the hood there are many modules that can be easily ported from this application to many other more complex applications.

Let's start by creating an overall layout (wireframe) of our application and see what the big picture looks like.

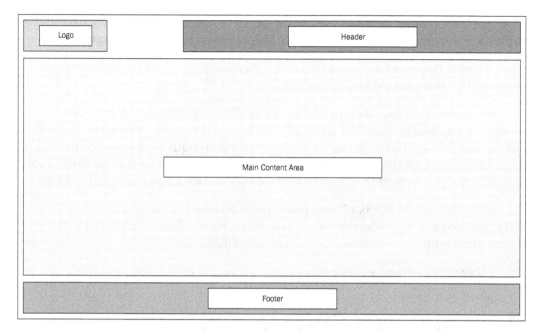

I have identified the main pieces of our index page in this mock-up. We are going to create modules to build and update this page, its related pieces, and the rest of the application for us.

Dynamic views

I mentioned that our JavaScript modules are going to build this page for us, and I need to explain this a little further.

While we are going to create modules to take care of the functional pieces of the application, we are going to take that a step further. We are also going to create modules that will specialize in building our pages (views) dynamically on the client side.

In this design, we only receive the skeleton of the page from the server. The page will be populated by our view-generating modules based on the object definitions for each page section (fragment) that is sent to the client.

The overall architecture of our application is based on **Single Page Application (SPA)** design concepts. If you are not familiar with this term, the idea is that as we navigate through our application pages (views), we won't need to load or build the parts of the page that don't change from one view to the next. We simply update the changed pieces of the view dynamically on the client while keeping the rest of the view untouched.

Since we only do targeted changes in our application's view, the rendering of our views will be more robust and optimized.

This also means that after the application's initial load, the client will only be requesting the changed parts of the application from the server. Therefore, we will only be transferring the page fragments over the bandwidth as opposed to the full page. Generally speaking, this can be a great advantage when we design applications that need to operate in limited bandwidth scenarios, such as mobile applications.

For our application in this book, our page fragments are transferred as object definitions to the client side and our view-generating specialized modules will render the required views based on such object definitions.

You will see how we can achieve this in the near future as we move forward.

Designing our SPA main pieces

Usually when designing SPA applications, I create a core application code base which is loaded in the browser at the application's initial load phase. This code base provides application-level functionality that is independent of the application's views. The application core consists of many modules that are loaded together. If you are familiar with **Model-View-Controller (MVC)** or **Model-View-Wildcard (MV*)** application design patterns, this core is essentially the controller of the application.

MVC and MV* design patterns

These design patterns create a good degree of specialization and separation of concerns in the code. Understanding these patterns is important in creating a good application architecture. While I will be referring to these patterns from time to time, covering them in depth is beyond the scope of this book.

I recommend the following resources for more information:

https://www.packtpub.com/application-development/mastering-javascript-design-patterns/

https://addyosmani.com/blog/understanding-mvc-and-mvp-for-javascript-and-backbone-developers/

The model and views of the application also have their own specialized modules, some of which are loaded at the initial application load time and some as needed, dynamically, at a later time. This type of approach enables the application to have a small footprint in the browser and load only what it needs, as needed.

I also usually try to have every page of my application as a separate module (component) both on the server and the client side. This provides the capability to create, modify, or remove pages (components) and their related code without affecting other pieces of the application.

Note that I'm using the term "module" here as a general term and it does not necessarily mean modules that are built using the module pattern. My intent is to convey the idea that each page is a separate piece in the application, within which one or many JavaScript modules can be used to do the work related to that page and that page only. If you are not sure exactly what this means, rest assured it will all become more clear to you shortly.

The following figure depicts the main pieces of our application for this book, categorized by their special functionality and design:

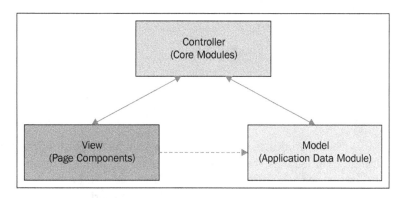

As the figure shows, our overall design is based on three main pieces: **Controller**, **View**, and **Model**. In the rest of this chapter, we will talk about each piece and will start building them based on our modular architecture.

Application controller

The controller is the piece that contains the main functionality of the application. Essentially, the controller module is the brain of the application. It will consist of application-level modules that provide application-level functionality. This piece will also be responsible for initializing all the other modules and components in the application as well as gluing them together using a loose coupling approach.

Application controller modules

Considering the role of the controller in our application as mentioned, we are going to design this piece based on specialized modules. These modules together create what we will be referring to as the **core** module.

Keep in mind that since we are using specialized modules for our core, each module can easily be modified or replaced without affecting the other parts of the application, that is, with the exception of the functionality that is related to that module and that module only.

Of course, we can also add more modules to the core, if we decide that additional functionality is needed at some point in the future.

It is the collective functionality of the controller modules that provides the core functionality of the application.

Based on our application's requirements, I anticipate that we will be needing the following modules in our application's controller:

- Page updater module
- Storage handler module
- Communication handler module
- Utilities module
- Message handler module
- Logging handler module

Keep in mind that we are making our best guess as to what modules are required. The list can change over time as we proceed further in our implementation. The idea is to design and implement the modules that we think we will be needing at this time, to have a starting baseline. However, the list of the modules, their functionality as well as the names that we choose for them can change over time.

Let's start by exploring what the functionality of each module in our application's core will be.

Page updater module

This module is responsible for building HTML pieces in our application. It does this task by injecting a string passed to it into a container. This string corresponds to the HTML elements that need to be rendered into the predefined container.

We will be building various pieces of our application pages and updating them dynamically as required, using this module.

Storage handler module

This module has the specific responsibility of storing application-related data. This data can be either stored in cookies or in other storage facilities provided by the browser, such as HTML 5 local storage.

Communication handler module

All application-related communication is done through this module. This module is mainly designed to use AJAX calls to communicate with the back-end server. However, the method of communication that this module uses might not be limited to AJAX calls at some point in the future.

Utilities module

This module is responsible for providing utility type functionality to the application. For instance, it can do string manipulation, object cloning, or page resize calculations.

Message handler module

As events take place in the application, we need a way to communicate such events with the users and display messages on the application's pages. This module specializes in this task.

Logging handler module

This module provides all the functionality related to the logging mechanism of the application. The logging can take place on the client side, the server side, or both.

Creating our first core module

Now that we have put together the list of possible required modules for the core, let's create the first module of our application's controller, the `PageUpdater` module. This module should be designed in such a way that it can dynamically update a fragment of the page. This fragment can be as small as a text on the page, or as large as the entire displayed page itself. The update to the page fragment can be as trivial as changing the font size or the background color or as complex as completely re-structuring and re-rendering of the page fragment altogether.

Structure of our first module

Consider the following:

```
var PageUpdater = (function(){

    // module private function
```

```
var insertHTMLTxt = function(containerID,newStructure){

    var theContainer = document.getElementById(containerID);
    theContainer.innerHTML = newStructure;
};

// module private function
var applyElementCSS = function(elementID, className){

    var theElement = document.getElementById(elementID);
    theElement.className = className;
};

return{

    // privileged method
    updateElement : function(elemID, htmlTxt){

        insertHTMLTxt(elemID,htmlTxt);
    },

    // privileged method
    updateElementClass : function(elemId,className){

        if(!className){

            console.error('No class name has been
                provided, exiting module!');
        }
        applyElementCSS(elemId,className);
    }
};

})();
```

The preceding code implements a simple module which enables us to do an update on a page fragment. Let's examine the code and see how it is structured.

We have defined a JavaScript module, using the module pattern. An IIFE is used to execute the code in our anonymous function, which creates a namespace. What gets returned from this function is an object that is assigned to our global variable `PageUpdater`.

In our IIFE, we have defined `insertHTMLTxt` and `applyElementCSS` method properties, using function expressions. These two methods are kept within the internal private scope of our main container function, and as such no external code can access them. Thus, we are protecting them from accidental and unintended modifications.

We do provide controlled and indirect access to these methods through the module's interface, which is the anonymous object that is returned when our container function is executed. A reference to this returned object (our module's interface) is assigned to the `PageUpdater` variable.

So in fact what is really referenced in this variable (`PageUpdater`) is the following object:

```
{
        // privileged method
        updateElement : function(elemID, htmlTxt){

            insertHTMLTxt(elemID,htmlTxt);
        },
        // privileged method
        updateElementClass : function(elemId,className){

            if(!className){

                console.error('No class name has been
                    provided, exiting module!');
            }
            applyElementCSS(elemId,className);
        }
    };
```

As this is just a normal JavaScript object, we can call its methods from the external code as:

```
PageUpdater.updateElement("headerContainer",
    headerContainerDef.sectionHTML);
```

The `updateElement` method of the `PageUpdater` object in turn calls `insertHTMLTxt(elemID,htmlTxt)`, which is the method inside our container function that does the real work behind the scene.

This method receives two parameters: the id of the container element (`containerID`), which we intend to update its contents, and a string (`newStructure`), which is the string representation of the HTML elements that will be rendered inside this container element.

If you are wondering how `PageUpdater` object can call the method inside of our container function and how the link is established between the two, you need to think of one word: closure!

We did talk about closures in *Chapter 2, Review of Important JavaScript OOP Concepts*. If you recall, because the anonymous object returned from our IIFE was defined inside the container function, it has access to the internal private scope of our container function. This means `PageUpdater` has access to all the private variables and methods defined inside of that scope. That is why the methods that are returned as part of the interface from the module are called, **privileged methods**.

Having problems understanding the module pattern?

I took some time here to explain our first simple module in depth. Moving forward, I will not be explaining the pattern used in creating our modules (module pattern) in as much detail. It is important for you to have a good understanding of this pattern, as our other modules in the application follow a similar structure.

For a better understanding of the module pattern, I recommend doing two things. First, review *Chapter 2, Review of Important JavaScript OOP Concepts* and *Chapter 3, Module Design Pattern* again. Second, spend some time analyzing the previous code and read my explanations a couple more times. I'm sure you will get a good grasp of this pattern very soon.

Note that the `PageUpdater` module is currently capable of doing two things. It can update the `innerHTML` of a container element as well as being able to update the **CSS class** of an element on the page.

Using our first module's functionality

The following is an example of how we can leverage the module's functionality by making calls to its methods:

```
PageUpdater.updateElement("footerContainer",
    footerContainerDef.sectionHTML);

PageUpdater.updateElementClass("footerParentContainer",
    "footerContainerClass_Test");
```

The first line of the preceding code populates the footer section of our application, based on a predefined object definition, which we will talk about a little later in this chapter. The second line of code changes the CSS class of the footer container to apply a different background color to this page fragment. The code accompanying this chapter has the CSS class definition for this operation.

As you can see, we let the module take care of the mechanics of how page fragments are updated, and all we have to do is to make simple calls to it through the interface that has been provided for this module.

Mapping our module's methods to its interface

There is one important point that we need to note regarding our module's interface, which can easily be missed.

If you recall, in *Chapter 3, Module Design Pattern*, I mentioned that a module is free to implement how it accomplishes its tasks and this implementation can change over time. However, a module should keep its interface consistent to the outside world. Of course, this is because the interface of a module is the module's contact and that's how the other pieces of the application can interact with it.

Notice how we have defined the following interface for our `PageUpdater` module:

```
updateElementClass : function(elemId,className){

        if(!className){

                console.error('No class name has been provided,
exiting module!');
        }
        applyElementCSS(elemId,className);
}
```

As you can see, to the outside world, when a CSS class needs to be applied to an element, the `updateElementClass` method should be called on the module. This module in turn calls a method with a different name in the module's definition, which is `applyElementCSS`.

This type of mapping allows us to change the name of the internal method of the module without affecting the module's interface for the external code. The mapping provides a layer of abstraction between the module's internals and its public interface.

Our module is currently a simple module that does relatively simple things for our application, but it does not have to be limited to what we have defined here.

As we move along in this book, we will be augmenting this module (and others) to do more things. Nonetheless, we should always keep in mind that this module is specialized to only do tasks that are related to updating of our application pages and nothing beyond that. After all, one of the main ideas behind modular design is that each module only does one type of work and nothing more so we can stay true to the concept of separation of responsibilities and concerns.

Running the accompanying application's code

You'll be able to run the application's code by loading the `index.html` page in the browser using any IDE that has a built in web server.

Please have a look at the code that accompanies this chapter and use this module to update different fragments of the page as you wish. All the modules discussed in this chapter can be found in the `js/Modules.js` file in the accompanying code.

Application view

Another main piece of our application is the **view** piece. As the name implies, this piece deals with the view of all the pages and page fragments of the application. The view is what the user actually sees in the browser.

Since our application is based on a MV* type architecture (in conjunction with modular architecture), our views interact with the controller as well as the model pieces.

However, the way we will build our application's views is a little different than traditional MV* applications. Our application views will be designed as modules and because these modules specialize in creating views, we will be calling them **components**. This is to make the distinction between modules that have views and those that only provide functionality but have no direct relations to our application's views.

One other thing to keep in mind about components is that they can implement their own MV* architecture. This type of implementation might not be very clear to you at this time, but I assure you that it will all make more sense in the following chapters.

In this section, we will only focus on how `index.html` is built and how it is populated using a few object definitions and the controller methods that we saw in the previous section.

To create our `index.html` page, we will start by building a skeleton for this page and then we will dynamically modify this skeleton to produce its main fragments.

Creating the index.html page skeleton

The page skeleton of our application is designed to be as minimalist as possible at this stage.

Have a look at the page structure as follows:

```html
<!DOCTYPE html>
<html lang="en">
<head>
    <meta charset="UTF-8">
    <meta content="width=device-width,
      initial-scale=1.0" name="viewport">
    <title>Images Inc.</title>
    <link href="css/app.css" rel="stylesheet">
</head>
<body>
    <header class="headerContainerClass"
      id="headerContainer" role="banner">
    </header>
    <main class="clearfix mainPageContainerClass"
      id="mainPageContainer" role=
    "main"></main>
    <div class="footerContainerClass" id="footerParentContainer">
        <div class="footerlinksContainerClass"
          id="footerContainer"></div>
    </div>
    <script src="js/Modules.js" type="text/javascript">
    </script>
</body>
</html>
```

When we render this HTML markup in the browser, we will have the following skeleton of our index.html page displayed:

Notice that we have created three main containers: `headerContainer` (the top section of the page), `mainPageContainer` (the middle section of the page), and `footerContainer` (the bottom section of the page), which are the three main fragments of the page.

We will be populating each one of these page fragments with the HTML elements that we need.

Creating an object definition for the header

If you recall, I mentioned that we will be using object definitions to define our page fragments in the application.

As these object definitions are very similar to each other, we will only examine one of them in this section , which is related to the header fragment of the page.

Here is the object definition for the header section:

```
var headerContainerDef = {
    sectionHTML: '<div class="logo_titleClass" >' +
        '<a href=""><img src="img/ImagesIncLogo.png"
          alt="Company Logo" style="max-height:100%;"></a>' +
        '<div class="siteTitleClass">Images Inc.</div>'
          + '</div>' +
        '<nav role="navigation" itemscope
           itemtype="https://schema.org/SiteNavigationElement">' +
        '<h1 class="hiddenClass">Main Navigation</h1>' +
        '<ul class="navmenuClass" >' +
        '<li><a href="#" class="active">Home</a></li>' +
        '<li><a href="#">Our Company</a></li>' +
        '<li><a href="#">Pricing</a></li>' +
        '<li><a href="#">Contact Us</a></li>' + '</ul>' + '</nav>'
};
```

As you can see, we have defined an object literal which at this time only contains one property, `sectionHTML`.

This property holds a string that is the string representation of the HTML elements for the header fragment of the page.

Keep in mind that, as implemented, we currently have a global variable called `headerContainerDef` for our object definition. As you know, we should try to avoid using global variables in our code. We will be fixing this issue soon, but at this time it is done so on purpose.

Now that we have created our first object definition, it is time to create the first view of our application for the Header fragment.

Generating the Header fragment dynamically

As you saw previously, our application's controller has a module that specializes in generating page fragments on the page and it is called `PageUpdater`.

Consider the following code snippet:

```
PageUpdater.updateElement("headerContainer",
    headerContainerDef.sectionHTML);
```

As you can see, we have used our application's `PageUpdater` module and have passed the id of the Header fragment as the first parameter to its `updateElement` method. The second parameter to this method is the object definition for the Header fragment. This implementation allows us to leverage the functionality of our application's controller to render the Header fragment.

Of course, we can use the same approach to create other parts (fragments) of our page, such as the footer, as follows:

```
PageUpdater.updateElement("footerContainer",
    footerContainerDef.sectionHTML)
```

The following screenshot shows how the `index.html` page for our application is displayed when the page fragments have been rendered on the page:

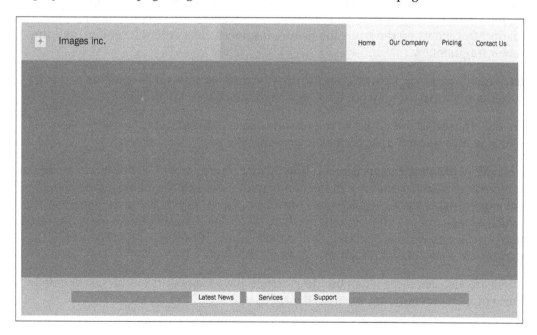

The main content area of the page (colored red in the middle of the page), is the area that will be updated as the user navigates through the pages in our application. The header and footer of the page will not be re-rendered for any of the application's pages, as our application is built on SPA principles.

As you can see, I have used some interesting background colors to depict each fragment of the page. I like to call this color-coding of the page fragments.

The reason for this coloring schema is to easily distinguish each specific region of the page in our visual design. When we are finished with our application implementation, this page will look a lot better, but for now, this is a good starting point.

Of course, if you are reading this book in a black and white medium, you only see light and dark shades in the preceding image.

Generating client application's view dynamically

One of the techniques that I use in my applications is what I call **Dynamic Page Generation (DPG)**.

The idea is that each main fragment of the page is associated with an object definition, and in this object definition the characteristics of the page fragment are defined. For instance, in our design for this application, I have considered three distinct fragments on the page: the header fragment, the content fragment, and the footer fragment.

Each main fragment, in turn, could further be divided into sub-fragments and each sub-fragment may or may not have its own distinct object definition.

On the other hand, we could have only one object definition for the entire page, which would be used to dynamically generate the page as a whole.

Generally speaking, the decision on how to associate an object definition to a page fragment or a sub-fragment is in the hands of the user interface developer. The developer makes these decisions by considering factors such as the frequency at which a fragment or sub-fragment needs to be updated, or whether a page fragment needs to be updated independently of other fragments of the page. Of course, performance also plays a major role in such decisions.

There are also instances when building certain page fragments on the server side is more robust than building them on the client.

In our application, we are building all the page fragments on the client dynamically. This is so we can explore the full functionality of our modules and components on the client side.

The look and feel of our application

Please note that the aim of this application is to help you understand the concepts of modular design as it relates to JavaScript applications, and as such the focus has not been on the look and feel.

While we will improve the appearance of the application as we move forward, I'm sure you can improve its appearance quite a bit further on your own. Our application is somewhat responsive based on the browser's view-port but can certainly use more CSS polishing to make it fully responsive.

However, I do consider this application as a **Minimum Viable Product** (**MVP**) for our purposes. Please feel free to download the code from the site that accompanies this book and improve it as you desire. Also, I have only tested this application in Chrome 46.0, but a production-quality application needs to be tested in a variety of different browser types and versions.

Application model

The last main piece of our MV* implantation is the model. The main role of this piece is to store application-level data. In a client application, such data can be stored in cache, in cookies, or in local or session storage.

In the main application for this book, we will be using most of such mechanisms to store our application's data. Also, as a general point, depending on the implementation of the MV* architecture, changes in the model's data can trigger changes in the application's view.

It is very important to shield application-level data from accidental overwrites and modifications. In our implementation, we are going to use the module pattern once again to create a module which will act as our application's model and will provide a good level of protection for the stored data.

Creating a module for our application's model

Consider the following implementation:

```
var GlobalData = (function(){

    var headerContainerDef = {

    sectionHTML :  '<div class="logo_titleClass" >' +
        '<a href=""><img src="img/ImagesIncLogo.png"
          alt="Company Logo" style="max-height:100%;"></a>' +
              '<div class="siteTitleClass">Images inc.</div>' +
        '</div>' +
        '<nav role="navigation" itemscope itemtype=
          "https://schema.org/SiteNavigationElement">' +
            '<h1 class="hiddenClass">Main Navigation</h1>' +
            '<ul class="navmenuClass" >' +
                '<li><a href="#" class="active">Home</a></li>' +
                '<li><a href="#">Our Company</a></li>' +
                '<li><a href="#">Pricing</a></li>' +
                '<li><a href="#">Contact Us</a></li>' +
            '</ul>' +
        '</nav>'
    };

    var footerContainerDef = {

        sectionHTML:'<div>' +
                '<a href="#">Latest News</a>' +
            '</div>' +
            '<div>' +
                '<a href="#">Services</a>' +
            '</div>' +
            '<div>' +
                '<a href="#">Support</a>' +
            '</div>'
    };

    return {

            getHeaderHTMLTxt: function(){
                return headerContainerDef.sectionHTML;
            },

            getFooterHTMLTxt: function(){
```

```
                    return footerContainerDef.sectionHTML;
            }
        };
    })();
```

As you can see, we have created a `GlobalData` module to keep our application-level data.

I'm sure you are pretty familiar with how the mechanism works by now. We have created an IIFE to return an object as an interface to our private namespace(module). This object provides two methods: `getHeaderHTMLTxt` and `getFooterHTMLTxt`.

These methods return the property values of two private variables `headerContainerDef` and `footerContainerDef` respectively.

Note that we have not provided any methods to set the values for these variables, and since they are private variables in our module, we have created a degree of encapsulation. Thus, shielding our data from outside influence.

The property value of `headerContainerDef` is a string representation of the HTML elements in the header fragment.

This string is used to populate the Header fragment of our application's view, as shown:

```
PageUpdater.updateElement("headerContainer",
    GlobalData.getHeaderHTMLTxt());
```

Just the same, the property value of `footerContainerDef` is a string representation of the HTML elements in the Footer fragment.

This string is used to populate the footer fragment of our application's view, as shown:

```
PageUpdater.updateElement("footerContainer",
    GlobalData.getFooterHTMLTxt());
```

Note that when we rendered our header and footer fragments previously, we used global variables (such as `headerContainerDef`) to get the required strings for the page fragments.

However, in our new implementation, we access these strings using the `GlobalData` interface methods.

An important point to keep in mind here is that we have implemented two independent modules (`PageUpdater` and `GlobalData`) that work together to create the building blocks of our application. We will leverage the collaboration among our application modules further as we advance through the next chapters, and will implement the full functionality of our application on such basis.

Also, notice that our `GlobalData` module is only tasked with providing data to other pieces of the application, and `PageUpdater` is only responsible for updating fragments of the page.

Another subtle point to consider is the fact that we can change the internals of both modules as we desire. But as long as the interfaces of the modules don't change, they can still continue working together without the internal changes of one module having any effect on the functionality of the other.

Creating a logging module

As a further exercise, we are going to create one more module in this chapter. This module will look after all the necessary work related to logging messages for our application.

The question is, which main application piece does this module belong to?

To answer this question, we need to do a simple analysis. First, since this module does not have any views associated with it, we need to consider it as a functional module and not a component.

Second, this module does not store any application data for us. Therefore, this module should belong to the controller piece of our application. As mentioned before, since we consider the controller piece of our application to be the same as the core module, the logging module should belong to the core module.

Remember that the core module consists of many smaller modules (sub-modules) that build the core together.

Let's create our simple logger module as follows:

```
var LoggingHandler = (function(){

    // module private variables
    var defaultHelloMsg = "this is just to say
      Hello to the users!",
    theInterface ={};

    // privileged method
    theInterface.logError = function(errorMsg){
        console.error(errorMsg);
    };
    // privileged method
    theInterface.logInfo = function(infoMsg){
```

```
        if(!infoMsg){
            infoMsg = defaultHelloMsg;
        }
        console.log(infoMsg);
    };

    return theInterface;

})();
```

This module definition structure is pretty much the same as other module definitions that we have seen so far, but with minor differences.

We have used a different technique here and have returned a named object instead of an anonymous object from our IIFE. We have named this object `theInterface`. Initially, this object is an empty object but then we augment this empty object with two method properties. One of them logs information messages and the other logs error messages to the console.

In the case that no information message is passed to `theInterface.logInfo` method, a default message is logged to greet the user.

Here is how we call the methods on the interface of this module:

```
LoggingHandler.logError("this is a test for logging errors!")
LoggingHandler.logInfo();
```

This is the same way that we call interface methods when we return an anonymous object from a module.

I have used this technique of returning a named object from a module here to show you we don't always have to return an anonymous object from an IIFE to create a module interface, and that there are different ways of implementing the module pattern. We will explore these techniques further in future chapters of the book.

Practical usage of our modules

As I like to present the concepts along with their practical aspects, I recommend that you download the accompanying code for this chapter. Have a look at the simple modules in action, and play around with the code as much as you can. This will help you become more familiar with the concepts and solidify them in your mind. My recommendation applies to this chapter as well as all the other chapters of the book.

Summary

In this chapter, we moved from the conceptual design of modules to the practical aspects of implementing them. We started by looking at the high-level requirements of our intended application, and then considered the kind of modules that we might possibly need to fulfill those requirements.

We briefly discussed the MV* design pattern and structured our application to follow this pattern. Then, based on the functionality and the role that our modules play in our design, we categorized them to be part of the controller, view or model pieces of our application.

The view for our application was generated by first creating an index.html page skeleton and then populating its main fragments based on object definitions, using a core module.

We also created a safe global data repository for our application to act as the model piece of our architecture.

An example of how modules can collaborate together to complete tasks and provide application level functionality was also presented.

In the next chapter we will extend our application modules and work further on the building blocks of our application in a modular design approach.

5
Module Augmentation

In the previous chapter, we started creating simple modules for our fictitious **Images Inc.** web application. In this chapter, we will take one of the modules that we have already built and add more functionality to it using an approach known as **module augmentation**.

This approach allows us to extend our modules without the need to change the original implementation. There are different techniques which can be used to implement module augmentation, and we will cover a couple of them in this chapter.

Module augmentation can be very useful when working on projects that have many contributors to the code base. This type of projects usually require us to extend our modules by adding new code and functionality to what has been already developed by other developers.

The concepts that we will cover in this chapter are:

- The idea behind module augmentation
- Loose augmentation
- Tight augmentation
- Generating our application's content area
- Module augmentation and script loading order
- Advantages and disadvantage of different augmentation techniques

Principles of module augmentation

As you saw in the previous chapter, we created specialized modules to do some specific tasks for us. However, as we move forward and develop our application further, we are going to require more functionality from our modules, and we will also require additional specialized modules.

When you are working on a large project, it is quite normal to have many developers working on various pieces of the application. It is also possible to have many developers work on the same part of the application together which requires a seamless approach for combining their efforts and the functionality that they add to the application.

Let's consider our `GlobalData` module from the previous chapter as an example. This module was responsible for storing and caching application-level data. However, in its current state, it holds a very limited amount of application-level data. It is quite feasible to assume that when different developers are working on other pieces of the application, they too need to store specific application-level data in the same module.

One way to do this, is by modifying the `GlobalData` module manually and adding more data and interfaces to it. But we need to keep in mind that the more people who modify the module, the higher possibility of something breaking in the module's code and for accidental modification to the important application-level data in an undesirable way.

On the other hand, the original module file may not be accessible to some developers for various reasons, which may hinder the cooperative development of our application.

What if we could come up with a way which would enable each developer to add the required functionality to the original module without the need to modify or require the original module's code?

Module augmentation allows us to do just that in a very robust way. As the name implies, this concept is about adding functionality (properties) to the original module, without changing the original module's code directly. The general idea is that we can create a namespace which imports the original module at runtime and then adds new functionality to it as required.

Implementing module augmentation

Imagine that we have a module called `ModuleA` and, as a developer, you want to add more functionality to this module. However, for some reason, you decide to implement this new functionality in a completely separate module and then dynamically augment the original module with all the data and capabilities of this new module. You can achieve this as shown here:

```
var ModuleA = (function(coreModule){
    var someData = "this is some data to be used later";
    coreModule.someMethod = function(){
        return someData;
```

```
    };

    return coreModule;
})(ModuleA);
```

As you can see, we are again using the module pattern here, as the intent is to add the new functionality in a modular fashion.

In this IIFE, a reference to `coreModule` object is returned.. There is, however, one important thing to keep in mind here. We are passing `ModuleA` as a parameter to our anonymous container function. Also, the property `someMethod` is being added to the passed-in `coreModule`, which is in fact a reference to `ModuleA`.

Therefore, at the end of this function execution, `ModuleA` has a new property method called `someMethod`, which has access to the value of `someData` variable.

There is one assumption that we are making here. We are assuming that `ModuleA` does exist as an object, and if not, we will get an execution error when we run the preceding code. You will see shortly how we can fix this issue, but for now, let's take this augmentation concept and use it to extend `ImagesInc_GlobalData` module in our application.

Module naming conventions

As we are getting more involved with module implementation in our application, it is best to use more specific naming for our modules. Generally speaking, it is a good idea to use names that are as specific as possible for our modules. This minimizes the chance of naming conflicts between our application modules and third-party modules that we might be loading in our application. For this reason, as we move forward, we will be adding `ImagesInc_` prefix to all of our module names, to make the names more specific to our application.

It is also worth mentioning that some developers choose to use all capital lettering for the name of their modules in the code, as a convention. We will not be using this convention in our application. In your own coding practices, whether to use all capital lettering for your module names or not is something that you should decide on with your team. This is so you can establish a set of standards which all the members of the team would be required to follow.

Simple augmentation of ImagesInc_ GlobalData

As you may recall, we used our `ImagesInc_GlobalData` module (previously named `GlobalData`) to store application-level data for us. This module also provided a couple of interfaces, so other pieces of the application could have access to the private data that we had stored in this module.

Let's create another JavaScript file, which adds more data and a new interface to this module. We can call this file `Modules_2.js` and add it to the list of JavaScript files that our main page loads at runtime, as follows:

```
<script type="text/javascript" src="js/Modules.js" ></script>
<script type="text/javascript" src="js/Modules_2.js" ></script>
```

As you can see, this file is added as any other JavaScript file would be in our `index.html`. However, one thing to notice in the preceding code is the order that the two module files have been added. This order is important and we will talk more about it shortly, but for now, keep in mind that our `ImageInc_GlobalData` module is loaded first in our application (as it resides in `Modules.js`). Then, the code residing in `Modules_2.js` will add more functionality to this module, as it is loaded afterwards.

We need to add the following lines of code to `Modules_2.js`:

```
(function(coreModule){

    coreModule.someText = "this is a test for
      module augmentation";
    coreModule.getExtendedModuleMsg = function(){
        ImagesInc_LoggingHandler.logInfo(coreModule.someText);
    };

})(ImagesInc_GlobalData);
```

Here, we have used an anonymous function to create a **namespace**, using an IIFE. We have also passed in a reference to the `ImagesInc_GlobalData` object (module) in the form of a parameter to this function.

Inside this anonymous function, we have added two properties to the passed-in object reference, `coreModule`. This means that our `ImagesInc_GlobalData` now has two new properties added to it. Let's verify this by running a test, as follows:

```
// displays "this is a test for module augmentation"
ImagesInc_GlobalData.getExtendedModuleMsg();
```

When we call `getExtendedModuleMsg` method on `ImagesInc_GlobalData` object, we see that the code runs properly and the expected message is shown in the console.

As the `ImagesInc_GlobalData` module did not originally have the method `getExtendedModuleMsg`, it now appears that it has been augmented with these new properties.

This simple example demonstrates how we can augment our original module without directly modifying the code in that module. We also saw that the augmentation can be done in a separate file, which means a different developer could add more functionality to our original module, without ever having direct access to the original module's code file.

Of course, this type of augmentation can just as easily be done when both the original module and the augmenting code are in the same file. It is good to have the flexibility to pick and choose which approach we would like to take: to either have the original module and its augmenting code in separate files or in the same file.

We will soon talk about this type of augmentation in greater depth, and will even give it a technical name.

The order of things in module augmentation

When we added `Modules_2.js` file to our `index.html`, I mentioned that we need to load this file after we load `Modules.js` file for things to work properly.

The reason for this is not hard to discover. If the order of loading these files is reversed, and subsequently the order of the code execution, we will be trying to add properties to an object (`ImagesInc_GlobalData`) that does not exist yet, which will result in a code execution error.

There are ways that we can work around this, which brings us to our next topic, **loose augmentation**.

Loose augmentation of modules

When we try to enhance a module using the augmentation technique previously discussed, we pass a reference of the module to another part of our code which is responsible for doing the augmentation work.

How can we add functionality to an object that has not been loaded or created yet?

The answer to this question becomes very important when our modules (files) are loaded in an asynchronous fashion, and we have no way of making sure that our original module is loaded before the augmentation code that enhances the module.

One of the beautiful and powerful aspects of JavaScript is its ability to add properties to objects dynamically, at any time during code execution. This allows us to add functionality or modify our original module's implementation even before the module is loaded, as long as we provide a temporary object in the absence of the module. This temporary object will be added to the original module after the module is loaded
(or more accurately, it becomes one with the original module).

If it sounds complicated, it really is simpler than you think. Let's revisit our previous augmenting code and examine it a little closer:

```
(function(coreModule){

    coreModule.someText = "this is a test for module augmentation";
    coreModule.getExtendedModuleMsg = function(){
        ImagesInc_LoggingHandler.logInfo(coreModule.someText);
    };

})(ImagesInc_GlobalData);
```

I mentioned that for the augmentation to work properly, we needed to load this code, which is responsible for augmenting the imageInc_GlobalData module, after the original module is loaded. Otherwise, a code execution error will be thrown. While that remains true, what if we compensate for when `ImagesInc_GlobalData` does not yet exist in the application by using an empty object?

As you probably know, we can call a function as follows:

```
someFunc(someParameter || someotherParameter);
```

When we do this, we are telling the JavaScript interpreter to pass `someParameter` when calling `someFunc`, if it has a value; and if not, pass `someotherParameter` to the function. That is how the || operator works in the preceding code snippet.

We can use the same technique and pass an empty object to our anonymous function, as follows:

```
(ImagesInc_GlobalData || {});
```

We tell the interpreter to pass a reference of our `ImagesInc_GlobalData` object when calling the function, if the object exists, or pass a reference of an empty object which will replace our original module for the time being.

Loose augmentation of ImagesInc_GlobalData

Let's rewrite our previous augmenting code for `ImagesInc_GlobalData` as follows:

```
var ImagesInc_GlobalData = (function(coreModule){

    coreModule.someText = "this is a test
        for loose module augmentation";
    coreModule.getExtendedModuleMsg = function(){
        ImagesInc_LoggingHandler.logInfo(coreModule.someText);
    };

    return coreModule;

})(ImagesInc_GlobalData || {});
```

In the preceding code, we are calling our anonymous function and passing a reference of `ImagesInc_GlobalData` to it, if `ImagesInc_GlobalData` does exist. Otherwise, we are passing a reference to an anonymous empty object into the function.

Our augmenting code still adds new properties to the passed-in object; however, this time it returns a reference to `coreModule` to the `ImagesInc_GlobalData` variable.

For everything to work properly, we also need to modify our original `ImagesInc_GlobalData` as follows:

```
var ImagesInc_GlobalData = (function(module){

    var headerContainerDef = {

    sectionHTML :  '<div class="logo_titleClass" >' +
                '<a href=""><img src="img/ImagesIncLogo.png"
alt="Company Logo" style="max-height:100%;"></a>' +
                '<div class="siteTitleClass">Images Inc.</div>' +
        '</div>' +
        '<nav role="navigation" itemscope itemtype="https://schema.
org/SiteNavigationElement">' +
            '<h1 class="hiddenClass">Main Navigation</h1>' +
            '<ul class="navmenuClass" >' +
                '<li><a href="#" class="active">Home</a></li>' +
                '<li><a href="#">Our Company</a></li>' +
```

```
                    '<li><a href="#">Pricing</a></li>' +
                    '<li><a href="#">Contact Us</a></li>' +
              '</ul>' +
        '</nav>'
    };

    var footerContainerDef = {

        sectionHTML:'<div>' +
                '<a href="#">Latest News</a>' +
            '</div>' +
            '<div>' +
                '<a href="#">Services</a>' +
            '</div>' +
            '<div>' +
                '<a href="#">Support</a>' +
            '</div>'
    };

    module.getHeaderHTMLTxt= function(){
        return headerContainerDef.sectionHTML;
    };

    module.getFooterHTMLTxt= function(){
        return footerContainerDef.sectionHTML;
    };

    return module;

})(ImagesInc_GlobalData || {});
```

As you can see, we have made a few modifications to the code.

If you recall, we used to create an anonymous object in our original module and return a reference to it like so:

```
return {

        getHeaderHTMLTxt: function(){
            return headerContainerDef.sectionHTML;
        },

        getFooterHTMLTxt: function(){
            return footerContainerDef.sectionHTML;
        }
    };
```

However, in our new augmenting implementation we are adding our module interface methods directly to the module object that is passed into the anonymous function. Also, the module object passed into our anonymous function is either a reference to `ImagesInc_GlobalData` or a reference to an empty object.

There is one other subtle point to notice here. Both the augmenting code and our original module code are returning an object reference to the `ImagesInc_GlobalData` variable, and this is very important.

To explain this point, we need to dig a little deeper. There are times in our applications that the module code and the code that is augmenting it are loaded asynchronously. This means that we cannot be sure ahead of time which code is executed first. When we return a reference to our object from both the original module and the augmenting code, we can be sure that regardless of the code execution order, our module is augmented properly.

In our example, if there is an `ImagesInc_GlobalData` object that already exists in the global namespace, we augment it with the new properties, and if not, we create it and then add new properties to it. That is why in both instances (the original module code and the augmenting code), we execute our IIFE with the following call:

```
(ImagesInc_GlobalData || {});
```

This provides us with the ability to create or augment our module in a non-strict order, hence the term **loose augmentation**.

Of course, the main advantage of this technique is that we don't have to worry about which file is loaded first; either way, our module is created and augmented as intended.

Keep in mind that in both cases, we need to make sure that we create the same global variable, `ImagesInc_GlobalData`, so that when we check for the existence of this object in the global namespace, the correct reference is passed in.

It is time to put our code to the test. After making the modifications mentioned previously, we can run the following line of code:

```
// displays "this is a test for module augmentation"
ImagesInc_GlobalData.getExtendedModuleMsg();
```

As you can see, the correct message is shown in the console. Now, let's see what happens if we change the order in which our JavaScript module files are loaded in the application.

First, we make the following change in our `index.html` file:

```
<script type="text/javascript" src="js/Modules_2.js" ></script>
<script type="text/javascript" src="js/Modules.js" ></script>
```

This is to make sure that our augmenting code is loaded first. Then we execute the same line of code as before:

```
// displays "this is a test for module augmentation"
ImagesInc_GlobalData.getExtendedModuleMsg();
```

We can see that both our original module and our augmenting code are working as expected, regardless of which was loaded and executed first.

Testing ImagesInc_GlobalData data encapsulation

We can test and see how encapsulation and privacy have been preserved in our module. This can be done by running the following code:

```
try{
        console.log(ImagesInc_GlobalData.headerContainerDef.
sectionHTML);

    }catch(e){
        ImagesInc_LoggingHandler.logError('could
          not access the property');
    }
```

This code will display **could not access the property** in the console, which confirms our original module encapsulation is still in effect, as we would like it to be.

A note about the project code

As always, I highly recommend that you download the related code for this chapter from the accompanying website for this book. In the code for this chapter, I have created a new file called AppTester.js, which is used to test the application as we modify and enhance it. I recommend this approach of testing our application every time we run it during the development phase. This is so we can be sure that our changes in one part do not cause any problems in other parts of the application. This is also aligned with **Test-Driven Development (TDD)** approach, but in a very rudimentary way.

Tight augmentation of modules

So far in this chapter, we have talked about what module augmentation is in general and have also covered the loose augmentation technique. It is time to explore a different technique used in augmenting modules, known as **tight augmentation**.

You might wonder if tight augmentation is the opposite of loose augmentation, and you are correct to think that, but with a couple of considerations which we will talk about a little later.

Tight augmentation is used for adding properties (functionality) to our modules when we do want to enforce a set order of file loading and code execution, and therefore it is less flexible. This type of augmentation is usually used when we need to make sure that a certain property from the original module is available for our augmenting code.

Tight augmentation of ImagesInc_GlobalData

Consider our augmenting code for `ImagesInc_GlobalData` module from the previous section, when loose augmentation was being used. As mentioned previously, since we are passing a reference to `ImagesInc_GlobalData` or an empty anonymous object into our IIFE, we can load our original module and our augmenting code in any order that we like.

This was shown as follows:

```
var ImagesInc_GlobalData = (function(coreModule){

    coreModule.someText = "this is a test for
      loose module augmentation";
    coreModule.getExtendedModuleMsg = function(){
        ImagesInc_LoggingHandler.logInfo(coreModule.someText);
    };

    return coreModule;

})(ImagesInc_GlobalData || {});
```

However, this also means that if we wanted to override one of the original module's properties, depending on what code gets loaded and executed first (the original module or the augmenting code), our "override" might be overridden by another piece of code, unintentionally and unexpectedly.

To understand this better, let's create another file, `Modules_3.js`, and add the following code to it:

```
var ImagesInc_GlobalData = (function(coreModule){

    coreModule.someText = "this is a test for overriding
        module properties with loose augmentation";
    coreModule.getExtendedModuleMsg = function(){
        ImagesInc_LoggingHandler.logInfo(coreModule.someText);
    };
    return coreModule;

})(ImagesInc_GlobalData || {});
```

Also, let's load this file in our application as follows:

```
<script type="text/javascript" async src="js/
    Modules_3.js" ></script>
<script type="text/javascript"    src="js/Modules_2.js" ></script>
<script type="text/javascript"    src="js/Modules.js" ></script>
```

Here we are loading two files (`Modules_3.js` and `Modules_2.js`), which augment our original module. `Modules_2.js` is being loaded before `Modules.js`, but `Modules_3.js` can be loaded in any order since we are using the `async` property on the `<script>` tag for this file. This property tells the browser to load the file in any order that it can.

Both of these augmenting codes add the same property, `coreModule.someText`, to the original module. However, depending on which code is loaded and executed first, only one of two pieces of text will be printed in the console.

We can test this by executing the following code:

```
ImagesInc_GlobalData.getExtendedModuleMsg();
```

The console will display one of the following:

- **this is a test for module augmentation** (from `Modules_2.js`)
- **this is a test for overriding module properties with loose augmentation** (from `Modules_3.js`)

Keep in mind that in this scenario, we have no control over which one of the strings will be the value of the `coreModule.someText` property after all the code execution is completed. This is because we don't know which augmenter code will be loaded and executed last. This also means that by using loose augmentation technique and asynchronous loading, augmenter code precedence is determined dynamically at runtime and not necessarily in the order that we think or desire.

On such basis, if our intent was that the value of `coreModule.someText` should be overridden by the code in `Modules_3.js`, then we could not be sure of such an override taking place.

Simulating asynchronous script loading

To simulate the asynchronous loading of our augmenters, you can reload the `index.html` page a few times in a row (from the application code accompanying this chapter). You'll see that the message displayed in the console may change from time to time. The message displayed depends on which file, `Modules_2.js` or `Modules_3.js`, is loaded first by the browser.

Tight augmentation, on the other hand, guarantees the order of code execution and therefore how our modules get augmented. By using this technique, we can be sure that when a module property is overridden, it will be in the order that we intended and the result will be as expected.

This guarantee is provided by the fact that we don't have any choice but to load our module and its augmenting code in the correct order, otherwise a code execution error will be generated.

Let's examine this by modifying the code in our `Moduels_3.js` as follows:

```
var ImagesInc_GlobalData = (function(coreModule){

    if(!coreModule){
        ImagesInc_LoggingHandler.logError('coreModule was
            not found to be augmented!');
        alert('coreModule was not found to be augmented!');
        return false;

    }

    coreModule.someText = "this is a test for overriding
        module properties with TIGHT augmentation";
    coreModule.getExtendedModuleMsg = function(){
        ImagesInc_LoggingHandler.logInfo(coreModule.someText);
    };

    return coreModule;

})(ImagesInc_GlobalData);
```

In this version of the augmenting code, we are no longer passing in a reference to an empty anonymous object to our IIFE. Therefore, if ImagesInc_GlobalData module has not been already loaded, we cannot augment it with any new properties.

Note that at the start of the preceding code we are checking to see whether coreModule exists, and if not we are using our ImagesInc_LoggingHandler module to log an error to the console. We are also using an alert box in the browser to make sure that the situation really catches the user's attention (try not to use alert boxes in production code as it looks unprofessional; I'm just using it here for ease of demonstration).

Loading ImagesInc_GlobalData augmenting code

To examine how tight augmentation enforces a set order of script loading and code execution, we can change our index.html as follows:

```
<script type="text/javascript"    src="js/Modules_3.js" ></script>
<script type="text/javascript"    src="js/Modules_2.js" ></script>
<script type="text/javascript"    src="js/Modules.js" ></script>
```

As you can see, we are no longer loading the Modules_3.js file asynchronously and it will be the first module-related file that gets loaded. Considering that we have modified the augmenting code in this file to only augment the module when the module (ImagesInc_GlobalData) is already present in the global scope, an error message will be logged and an **alert box** will be displayed in the browser when we load the page.

Because we are using the tight augmentation technique now, we need to load this augmenting code after either Modules.js or Modules_2.js. This is necessary so we can be sure that the ImagesInc_GlobalData module (object) is already present in the global scope.

Also, since our intention is to override the value of someText by using the code in Modules_3.js, and this property was added to the module by the augmenting code in Modules_2.js, we need to load both Modules.js and Modules_2.js first. This is the only way we can guarantee that an override of the value of someText is taking place as intended.Therefore, to achieve the proper override, we need to modify the loading order of our scripts as follows:

```
<script type="text/javascript"    src="js/Modules.js" ></script>
<script type="text/javascript"    src="js/Modules_2.js" ></script>
<script type="text/javascript"    src="js/Modules_3.js" ></script>
```

This rearrangement of the order of scripts in our `index.html` file ensures that the override of the value of the `someText` property for the module will produce the expected result. This is of course, because our original module is loaded first, then it is augmented with the `someText` property, using the augmenting code in `Modules_2.js`. At the end, the value of this property is overridden by the tight augmenting code in `Module_3.js`.

Considerations in tight augmentation

At the beginning of this section, I mentioned that there are a couple of considerations regarding tight augmentation that we need to keep in mind.

First, we do not really need to create a global variable to store the returned value from the augmenting code that implements the tight augmentation technique.

This is so since this type of augmentation can only take place if the module already exists in the global context. In fact, the following code will work just as well as the previous version:

```
(function(coreModule){

    if(!coreModule){
        ImagesInc_LoggingHandler.logError('coreModule was
            not found to be augmented!');
        alert('coreModule was not found to be augmented!');
        return false;

    }

    coreModule.someText = "this is a test for overriding
        module properties with TIGHT augmentation!!!";
    coreModule.getExtendedModuleMsg = function(){
        ImagesInc_LoggingHandler.logInfo(coreModule.someText);
    };

})(ImagesInc_GlobalData);
```

Second, before we override a property that already exists in the module, we can preserve the original value of the property by storing it in another property. This allows us to have access to both the original value of the property and its overridden value.

Let's do that in our `Modules_3.js` file, as follows:

```
(function(coreModule){

    if(!coreModule){
        ImagesInc_LoggingHandler.logError('coreModule was not found to
be augmented!');
        alert('coreModule was not found to be augmented!');
        return false;

    }

    coreModule.original_someText = coreModule.someText;

    coreModule.someText = "this is a test for overriding module
properties with TIGHT augmentation!";

    coreModule.getExtendedModuleMsg = function(){
        ImagesInc_LoggingHandler.logInfo(coreModule.someText);
    };
    coreModule.getExtendedModuleOriginalMsg = function(){
        ImagesInc_LoggingHandler.logInfo(coreModule.original_
someText);
    };

})(ImagesInc_GlobalData);
```

We can get the original value of the `someText` property by running the following in the console:

```
// displays ""this is a test for module augmentation"
ImagesInc_GlobalData.getExtendedModuleOriginalMsg();
```

As you can see, not only tight augmentation technique is a nice way to override our module properties, it also allows us to hold on to the original (previous) values of our properties, in case we ever need to use them again.

Generating our application's content area

If you have read the previous sections of this chapter, you have a pretty good grasp of what module augmentation is by now. You also know of a couple of techniques to add dynamic properties to our modules using augmentation.

As it stands, our application (`Images Inc.`) has code that dynamically generates the header and footer sections of our pages. But we still have an empty space in the middle (the content area), which needs to be populated with content.

Let's put the techniques that we have learned in this chapter to good use and add functionality to our application that will generate the content area dynamically.

Note that the refactored augmenting code in Modules_3.js is now as follows:

```
(function(originalModule){

    if(!originalModule){
        ImagesInc_LoggingHandler.logError('originalModule
            was not found to be augmented!');
        return false;
    }

    //object definition for the index.html content area
    originalModule.mainContentContainerDef = {
        sectionHTML: (function(){
            var htmlStr = "";

            for(var i=0; i<=15; i++){
                htmlStr += '<div class="productDiv"></div>';
            }
            return htmlStr;
        })()

    };

    originalModule.getContentAreaHTMLTxt= function(){
        return originalModule.mainContentContainerDef.sectionHTML;
    };

})(ImagesInc_GlobalData);
```

A few things have happened here. As you can see, we are using tight augmentation to augment our ImagesInc_GlobalData module. We have also created a new property for this module, originalModule.mainContentContainerDef, which holds the object definition for the content area of the page. Since the content area uses a repeated structure of rectangles to display the desired images on the page, we have used an inner IIFE, which creates that structure and stores it in sectionHTML property of the content area object definition as a string.

In order for the external code to have access to this string, and to be able to render the content area of our index.html page, we have created originalModule. getContentAreaHTMLTxt method. This is added as an interface to our original ImagesInc_GlobalData module.

When we load the application's `index.html` page now, it is displayed as shown here:

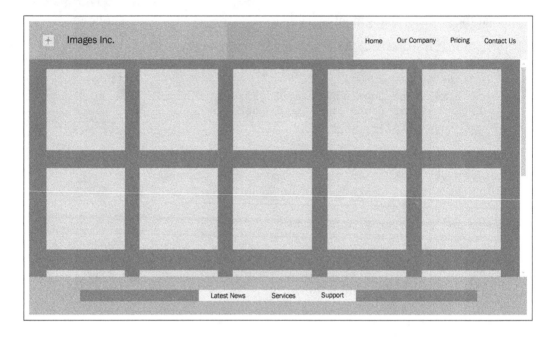

Of course, for the time being, I'm using the previous color coding schema that you have seen before for our various page fragments. For ease of identification, the image boxes are shown in pink (if you are reading the book in color).

A caveat to keep in mind

In our augmenting code, we added the `mainContentContainerDef` property to our module without using a closure. Therefore, this property is not implemented with the same type of encapsulation and private access as `headerContainerDef` and `footerContainerDef`. These properties were defined in our original module as private variables, and access to them was only possible through the interfaces that we created for external use. Of course, we created that private access using a closure.

If you'd like to restrict access to them in your modules, it is best to define the properties in the original modules (using closures) as opposed to adding them to the modules using the augmentation techniques (unless you use closures in your augmenting code too).

Summary

In this chapter, we covered what module augmentation is and explored a couple of different techniques, known as loose augmentation and tight augmentation, to implement module augmentation.

We saw how each approach is used in different circumstances and for different application requirements, as well as the pros and cons related to each technique.

The order in which scripts should be loaded was also discussed, based on the augmentation technique used.

Once we had a good grasp of these augmentation implementations, we refactored part of our application code to augment `ImagesInc_GlobalData` module. Subsequently, we generated the content area of `index.html` page and populated it with containers, which will host the images for our application in the future.

In the next chapter, we will look at some more techniques in modular design which will enable us to extend and clone our modules as needed.

6
Cloning, Inheritance, and Submodules

In the previous chapter, we looked at how we can extend and modify modules using loose and tight augmentation.

In this chapter, we are going to explore some other techniques that may come handy when we are working with modules, which can help us extend and modify the functionality of our modules. Depending on the requirements of your applications, as well as your personal preferences, some or all of these techniques may be of use to you.

The beginning of the chapter will provide an overview of some of the approaches for creating object based on other objects which you may already be familiar with. Then, we will look at how object cloning can be used to create objects that are replicas of other objects.

We will also create another one of the core modules for our application, which will be utilized to clone objects as needed.

In this chapter we will cover:

- Module cloning and when to use it
- Different methods for cloning objects
- Using inheritance to extend modules
- Adding functionality to already created modules using submodules
- Internal private state and how it is affected when extending modules

Cloning modules

Cloning objects in general, and cloning modules in particular, is about creating an exact replica of the original object or module.

But before we talk about cloning, let's consider some of the ways that we can create new objects based on other objects.

Creating instances of a constructor function

One way of creating objects based on another object is by creating instances of a constructor function.

As you know, when we create an instance of an object using a constructor function in JavaScript, we use the new keyword. The created instance resides in a different memory address than the constructor function. When we assign properties to the prototype property of the constructor function, all the instances of the constructor function will share these properties of the prototype object.

Let's have a look at a simple example and review creating objects based on constructor functions.

Consider the following code snippet:

```
function testConstructor (){

    this.someValue = "Value in the constructor function";

}

testConstructor.prototype.testFunc = function(){

    console.log(this.someValue);
};
```

As you can see, we have added a property to the prototype object of our constructor function, which logs the value of the this.someValue property to the console.

Now, we create two instances of our constructor function as follows:

```
var firstInstance = new testConstructor();
var secondInstance = new testConstructor();
```

Next, we run the following code in the console:

```
// displays "Value in the constructor function"
console.log(firstInstance.someValue);
// displays "Value in the constructor function"
console.log(secondInstance.someValue);
```

We can see that the same value for `someValue` property will be displayed for both of the instances. Of course, if we change the value of `someValue` property for each instance as follows:

```
firstInstance.someValue = "value for the firstInstance";
secondInstance.someValue = "value for the secondInstance";
```

And log the values of the properties:

```
// displays "Value for the firstInstance"
firstInstance.testFunc();
```

```
// displays "Value for the secondInstance"
secondInstance.testFunc();
```

The value of `someValue` property for each instance will be different. Here, each instance has its own copy of `someValue` property, but they both share the same method, (`testFunc`) since all the properties that are residing on the `prototype` object are shared among all the instances of the constructor function.

There is also one more thing that we should keep in mind. After creating instances of the constructor function, if we add new properties to the constructor function, the instances will not have access to these new properties.

Consider the following code:

```
testConstructor.newProperty = "this is a new property but not shared";
```

```
// displays undefined
console.log(firstInstance.newProperty);
```

```
// displays undefined
console.log(secondInstance.newProperty);
```

As you see, none of the instances have access to this new property which was added to the constructor function **after** the instances were created.

If you are thinking that alternatively, we could have defined properties defined on the `prototype` object directly on the constructor function itself (`testFunc` in our example), you are correct but with a caveat!

Doing so would mean that every time we make an instance of the object, we would be making unnecessary copies of the properties, which are identical for all the instances of the object. Thus, we would be creating an unnecessary overhead for our code.

It is a good practice that, when we have properties which are identical for all the instances of constructor function (in most cases, this applies to methods), they should be defined on the `prototype` object and be shared among all the instances. We did this in our example by adding `testFunc` method to the `prototype` object instead of defining it on the constructor function itself.

When it comes to constructor functions and creating other objects (instances) based on these objects, there is one other thing that we need to consider. What happens to private properties in the constructor function?

Let's consider the following code snippet:

```
function testConstructor (){
    this.someValue = "Value in the constructor function";
    var privateValue = "no instances will have a copy of me";
}
```

The private variable `privateValue` will not be copied to the instances of the object and will not be shared.

We can test this as follows:

```
var firstInstance = new testConstructor();
// displays undefined.
console.log(firstInstance.privateValue);
```

So how can we access these private properties from an object which is created based on this object?

We'll talk about how we can provide access to such private members when we talk about cloning modules.

Using the assignment operator for copying objects

When we are using primitive types in JavaScript, we can easily use the assignment operator to copy the value of one variable to another, as shown:

```
var testVar1 = "This is to be copied";
var testVar2 = testVar1;
```

In the preceding code we are simply assigning the sting value of one variable to another variable, and there is no mystery here, but how would that work for two objects?

Let's put that to the test as follows:

```
var testObj1 = { testValue : 5};
var testObj2 = testObj1;

testObj1.newValue  = "this is a new value";

// displays "this is a new value"
console.log(testObj2.newValue);
```

Here, we are assigning testObj1 to testObj2 using the assignment operator, which might appear as creating a new object based on another object.

However, as you can see, when we create a new property for testObj1, even after the assignment of testObj1 to testObj2 has taken place, the new property is available to testObj2 as well.

The reason is that when we use the assignment operator to assign the value of a variable which holds a reference to an object to another variable, we are in fact assigning the memory address of the object to another variable. This results in both variables referencing the same object. So, in the code above, both testObj1 and testObj2 are referencing the same object.

While this result might be desirable at times, there are occasions when we need to create an object that is an exact copy (replica) of another object, but we want the new object to be a completely independent object from the original one. So how do we do that?

One way to achieve that is to create a clone of the original object.

Creating a clone of an object

When we create a clone of an object, our objective is to create an exact replica of the original object, without the newly created object having any ties to the original object.

Cloning objects in JavaScript (as with some other languages) is not as straightforward as you might think. While there are different ways of implementing cloning, each approach has its own pros and cons.

If we consider cloning as copying all the properties of an object to another object, we can categorize cloning into two types:

- Shallow cloning
- Deep cloning

Shallow cloning and deep cloning

Shallow cloning copies all the top-level properties of the original object, but if this object contains other reference types, only the *references* of these reference types are copied to the newly created clone, as opposed to the actual reference types. This type of cloning is used when we want to have separate copies of the primitive types in the new object but we want the original object, and the newly cloned object, to share the same reference types.

Deep Cloning on the other hand, copies all the primitive type properties of the original object into the new object as well as making new copies of all the reference types of the original object in the new object.

The important distinction is that true copies of the reference types are created in the new object and not just the references (the memory addresses) of the reference types. This type of cloning is desirable if we want to have two distinct objects with no ties between them of any kind. Deep cloning is generally considered slower than shallow cloning and consumes more resources.

To implement either of the cloning types, we can leverage one of the following approaches:

- Use a third-party library such as jQuery or lodash
- Use the JSON exploit hack
- Create our own custom clone method

Using external libraries for cloning

jQuery provides the `extend` method which enables us to create both shallow and deep cloning of objects.

The general format for the `extend` method is as follows:

```
jQuery.extend( target [, object1 ] [, objectN ] );
```

While this approach is generally a good option for cloning objects, it does have some limitations, such as when dealing with built-in JavaScript types. For complete information regarding this method, please refer to the jQuery documentation at the following URL:

`http://api.jquery.com/jQuery.extend/`

Another good library that can be used for cloning of objects is **lodash**, which also provides functionality for both shallow and deep cloning. The cloning functionality that lodash provides seems to be ideal for most cases.

The general format for creating deep clones of an object in lodash is:

```
var deep = _.cloneDeep(objects);
```

 There are however some limitations when using lodash for deep cloning, such as dealing with maps and sets. Please refer to the loadash documentation online at:

`https://lodash.com/docs#cloneDeep`

Using JSON exploit for cloning

A simple but effective way of cloning objects is to use a technique (hack) known as JSON exploit.

The idea is to stringify the original object and then parse the string into a new object, using JSON methods. This is shown as follows:

```
var cloneObj = (JSON.parse(JSON.stringify(originalObj)));
```

 This approach is simple to use, however it has limited capabilities, especially when it comes to copying function properties.

To view a good discussion on using this technique, please refer to the following URL:

`https://esdiscuss.org/topic/deep-cloning-objects-defined-by-json`

Creating a custom clone method

When it comes to relatively simple cloning of objects, we can create our own custom cloning method. This method satisfies most of our needs, most of the time.

Consider the following:

```
function clone(deep) {
    var newClonedObj = new this.constructor();
    for (var property in this){
        if (!deep){
            newClonedObj[property] = this[property];
        }else if (typeof this[property] == 'object'){
            newClonedObj[property] = this[property].clone(deep);
        }else{
            newClonedObj[property] = this[property];
        }
    }
    return newClonedObj;
}
```

This function takes a Boolean parameter to perform either a shallow clone or a deep clone of an object.

When a deep clone is required, a recursive call to the function is made to copy the properties of an object property (a reference type) of the original object. Notice the following snippet in the cloning function:

```
else if (typeof this[property] == 'object'){
        newClonedObj[property] = this[property].clone(deep);
}
```

Of course, as with the approaches discussed previously, this approach also has its own limitations, for instance, when dealing with closures. However, it does a pretty good job in most cases.

In the next section, we will be adding this function to one of our application's core modules so it can be used in our application, when needed.

Creating ImagesInc_Utilites module

Since a utilities module is a good place to implement our object cloning code, let's create our `ImagesInc_Utilites` module as follows:

```
var ImagesInc_Utilitizes = (function(){

    var clone = function clone(deep) {

        // create an instance of the object
```

```
        var newClonedObj = new this.constructor();

        //copy all properties from the original object
        for (var property in this){
            // if deep flag is not set, just do a
              shallow copy of properties
            if (!deep){
                if(this.hasOwnProperty(property)){
                    newClonedObj[property] = this[property];
                }
            // to make a deep copy, call the function recursively
            }else if (typeof this[property] == 'object' &&
              this.hasOwnProperty(property)){
                newClonedObj[property] =
                    this[property].clone(deep);
            }else if(this.hasOwnProperty(property)){
                //Just copy properties for non objects
                newClonedObj[property] = this[property];
            }
        }

        return newClonedObj;
    };

    // attach the clone function to Object prototype
    var initialize  = (function(){
        Object.prototype.clone = clone;
    })();

})();
```

In this module, we have implemented our cloning function which takes care of copying an object's properties into a new object. I have also modified this function a little from its previous version that you saw earlier. This is so it will only copy the properties of the object itself and not its parent's properties (if there is one). We can do this by using JavaScript's native `hasOwnProperty` method.

We have assigned the cloning function as a property to `Object.prototype` object, so all the objects in the application can have access to this method.

Testing our custom cloning method in ImagesInc_Utilites module

Let's create a test module to see how our cloning mechanism works. Consider the following code:

```
var TestModule = (function(){

    var privateTestValue = "Test for cloning, this
      property is hidden";

    return {
        publicTestValue: privateTestValue + " but now
          showing it publicly",

        testFunc : function(){

            var anotherTest= "This property will be cloned";
            return anotherTest;
        },

        getPrivteValue : function(){

            return privateTestValue;
        },

        changePrivateVar : function(){
            privateTestValue = "the private value
              has been changed";

            return privateTestValue;

        },

        testArray : [1,2,3]
    };

})();
```

Here we have created a simple module which exposes a public interface with controlled access to its private variable.

Now, if we run the following code:

```
// creating a clone object
CloneModule = TestModule.clone(true);
```

We can create a clone of the original module, `TestModule`.

We can run a simple test as follows:

```
// displays "This property will be cloned"
console.log(CloneModule.testFunc());
```

As you can see, the expected output is displayed.

To verify that all the properties have been copied from our original module to our new module, we can examine all the properties in both modules, using our browser's debugger (I'm using Chrome's debugger) as shown here:

```
> TestModule
  ▼Object {publicTestValue: "Test for cloning, this message is hidden but now showing it publicly", testArray: Array[3]}
    ▶ changePrivateVar: function ()
    ▶ getPrivteValue: function ()
      publicTestValue: "Test for cloning, this message is hidden but now showing it publicly"
    ▶ testArray: Array[3]
    ▶ testFunc: function ()
    ▶ __proto__: Object
> CloneModule
  ▼Object {publicTestValue: "Test for cloning, this message is hidden but now showing it publicly", testArray: Array[3]}
    ▶ changePrivateVar: function ()
    ▶ getPrivteValue: function ()
      publicTestValue: "Test for cloning, this message is hidden but now showing it publicly"
    ▶ testArray: Array[3]
    ▶ testFunc: function ()
    ▶ __proto__: Object
```

An important aspect of our cloning method

There is also another interesting aspect of this cloning method that you need to be mindful of.

Remember that our `TestModule` has a hidden property by design, which is `privateTestValue`. What happens to this property when we do our cloning?

Well, the best way to find out is by running a test.

In our `TestModule`, we have a method property (`changePrivateVar`) which modifies this hidden property. So if we run the following:

```
// displays "the private value has been changed"
console.log(TestModule.changePrivateVar());
```

We can change the value of this property to the private value has been changed, in our `TestModule`. Now, let's see if our `CloneModule` has access to this value and if so, does it hold on to the old value of this property or will the value will be changed for our `CloneModule` as well?

If we run the following code snippet:

```
// displays "the private value has been changed"
console.log(CloneModule.getPrivteValue());
```

We see that not only our `CloneModule` has access to this property but also that the value has been changed for this module.

This shows us that because of the closure in our original `TestModule` module, our `CloneModule` also has access to the private scope of this module and it also retains the state of the scope that is provided by the closure.

This may, or may not, be a desirable result for us, depending on how we want to clone our modules. However, it is very important to keep in mind that, because of the closure in our original module, our cloning outcome is a little different than when we clone objects which do not have embedded closures.

Running more tests on our cloning method

I have included a few tests for module cloning in the accompanying code for this chapter. You can see these tests in the `AppTester.js` file. Please have a look, read the comments and modify the code to see how the results can be affected.

As you can see, cloning can be used when we want to create a replica of our original module with access to the original module's closure context. This in turn can provide us with access to the private members of the original module.

Most of the time, when we clone a module, we use it as the base module for a new module. We can then add more functionality or modify the existing functionality of the new module, using one of the other techniques that we discussed previously, such as loose or tight augmentation.

This approach allows us to extend the clone of a module instead of the original module, thus shielding the original module from all the changes, while having access to all the functionality of the original module.

Of course, cloning is not the only way that we can achieve this, but nonetheless, it is another valuable tool to have in our toolbox.

Inheritance in modules

In *Chapter 2, Review of Important JavaScript OOP Concepts,* we talked about what inheritance is and looked at different approaches to creating inheritance relationship among objects. Here, we will leverage the techniques that we learned in that chapter to create inheritance among modules.

Generally, we use inheritance to utilize our base module's functionality and then either add new functionality or modify the existing functionality in our child modules.

There are various ways of creating inheritance among modules and we will examine two of these approaches in this section.

Module inheritance using __proto__ object

In this type of inheritance implementation, we use the child module's __proto__ object to inherit properties from the parent module.

Let's consider the following:

```
var Polygon_Module = (function() {

    var sides = 6;
    var name = "Polygon";
    var type = "2D";

    function getSides() {

        return sides;
    };

    function getName() {

        return name;
    };

    function getType(){

        return type;
    };

    return {
```

```
            getSides: getSides,
            getName: getName,
            getType: getType
        };
    })();

    var Rectangle_Module = (function() {
        var Rectangle = {};
        var sides = 4;
        var name = "Rectangle";
        var color = "blue";

        Rectangle.__proto__ = Polygon_Module;

        Rectangle.getName = function(){
          return name;
        };

        Rectangle.getSides = function(){
          return sides;
        };

        Rectangle.getColor = function(){
            return color;
        };


      return {
          getName: Rectangle.getName,
          getSides: Rectangle.getSides,
          getType: Rectangle.getType
      };

    })();
```

As you can see, we have created two modules here: `Polygon_Module`, which is the parent module in our inheritance relationship, and `Rectangle_Module`, which is the child module.

In our `Polygon_Module`, we have created private variables and functions, which are not accessible to the external code, except through the module's interface.

`Rectangle_Module` is designed in a way that it inherits some of its functionality from its parent module (`Polygon_Module`). It then modifies some of the inherited functionality as well as adding new functionality of its own.

The following line of code is the essential piece that creates the inheritance relationship between the two modules:

```
Rectangle.__proto__ = Polygon_Module;
```

As shown, we have passed a reference from `Polygon_Module` to the `__proto__` object of `Rectangle` object. This allows the `Rectangle` object to have access to all the properties that were exposed in the parent module, through the parent module's interface.

Let's see what we get when we run the following tests on our modules:

```
console.log(Polygon_Module.getName()); //displays "Polygon"
console.log(Polygon_Module.getSides()); // displays 6
console.log(Rectangle_Module.getName()); // displays "Rectangle"
console.log(Rectangle_Module.getSides()); // displays 4
console.log(Rectangle_Module.getType()); // displays "2D"
```

The above tests demonstrate that the child module, `Rectangle_Module`, has all the methods that were inherited from the parent module; additionally, it has overridden some of these inherited properties.

Notice `Rectangle_Module.getType()` method, which was not defined or overridden in the child module, but was accessed by the child module through the parent module's interface.

Module inheritance using parasitic combination

Another approach to creating inheritance among objects, which you are probably familiar with and have seen an example of in *Chapter 2, Review of Important JavaScript OOP Concepts*, is **parasitic combination** inheritance.

As you may recall, the idea is that we use the base class's constructor function in the child's constructor to create an instance of the child object. We also use the base class's `prototype` object to get a reference to all the properties that are exposed on the base class's `prototype` object.

To refresh your memory, let's have a look at the following example:

```
var Polygon_Module2 = (function() {

    var sides = 6;
    var name = "Polygon";
    var type = "2D";

    function Polygon(){

        this.sides = sides;
        this.name = name;
        this.type = type;
    }

    Polygon.prototype.getSides = function(){

        return this.sides;
    };

    Polygon.prototype.getName = function(){

        return this.name;
    };

    Polygon.prototype.getType = function(){

        return this.type;
    };

    return {
        Polygon: Polygon,
    };
})();


var Rectangle_Module2 = (function(){
    var sides = 4;
    var name = "Rectangle";

    function Rectangle(){

        Polygon_Module2.Polygon.apply(this);
        this.sides = sides;
```

```
        this.name = name;
    }

    Rectangle.prototype = Polygon_Module2.Polygon.prototype;
    Rectangle.prototype.constructor = Rectangle;

    var RectangleInstance = new Rectangle();

    return {

        Rectangle: RectangleInstance
    };

})();
```

In this version of our modules, `Polygon_Module2` has a constructor function called `Polygon`. All of our methods are also defined on the `prototype` object of the `Polygon` class (object).

`Polygon_Module2` module also has an anonymous object as an interface, which holds a reference to `Polygon` class (object).

In our child module, we have created another constructor function `Rectangle`, which uses the available interface in `Polygon_Module2` to borrow the `Polygon` constructor, as shown:

```
    Polygon_Module2.Polygon.apply(this);
```

We have also set the `prototype` object of `Rectangle` object to point to `Polygon.prototype` object so we can have access to all the methods defined in this object, as shown:

```
    Rectangle.prototype = Polygon_Module2.Polygon.prototype;
    Rectangle.prototype.constructor = Rectangle;
```

And of course, since we have completely overwritten the `prototype` object of our `Rectangle` class, we need to reset its `constructor` property so that it points to the correct object, which in this case is `Rectangle`.

Notice that we have created an instance of `Rectangle` object to start the inheritance relationship between the two objects and set the objects' contexts properly.

Let's run a few tests to verify the inheritance relationship, as follows:

```
console.log(Rectangle_Module2.Rectangle.getName()); //
    displays "Rectangle"
console.log(Rectangle_Module2.Rectangle.getSides()); // displays 4
console.log(Rectangle_Module2.Rectangle.getType()); //
    displays "2D"
```

As you can see, the tests produce the results that were expected.

Deciding on the module inheritance approach

If you are wondering which approach to take (__proto__ **inheritance** or **parasitic inheritance**) when you need to create an inheritance relationship among your application modules, in my opinion it will be a matter of taste for the most part.

However, consider that in our first approach (using __proto__ inheritance), we did not need to create an instance of the child module to create the inheritance relationship. This means one less function call and probably a little less memory consumption as no instances of the object are held in memory.

On the other hand, keep in mind that older browsers may not support setting the __proto__ property of an object.

More information about inheritance

If you would like to get a little more information regarding inheritance among JavaScript objects in general, please refer to *Chapter 2, Review of Important JavaScript OOP Concepts*.

Submodules

The last technique that we consider in this chapter, which also allows us to extend our modules, is using **submodules**.

Submodules are essentially independent modules, which can be added to another module as properties of the hosting module. There are various ways of adding submodules to other modules and we will cover two of these approaches in this section.

Let's stay with the shape theme that we have been using so far and create a Shape module. We will consider this module as our hosting module. This module is the parent module for all 2D and 3D shapes and we will add our Polygon module to it.

Adding submodules using dynamic properties

Adding a submodule to a module as a dynamic property is straightforward, and as we can add dynamic properties to any JavaScript object, we can add a property to a hosting module which points to a submodule.

Consider the following:

```javascript
var Shape = (function(){

        var type = "Any 2D and 3D shape";

        function getType(){
            return type;
        }

        return {

            getType: getType
        };

})();

Shape.Polygon = (function() {

    var sides = 6;
    var name = "Polygon";
    var type = "2D";

    function getSides() {

        return sides;
    }

    function getName() {

        return name;
    }

    function getType(){

        return type;
```

```
        }

    return {
        getSides: getSides,
        getName: getName,
        getType: getType
    };
})();
```

Here, we have created a submodule Shape.Polygon and have added it to our main module Shape as a property.

Of course, we can access the main module and the submodule as follows:

```
console.log(Shape.getType()); // displays "Any 2D and 3D shape"
console.log(Shape.Polygon.getName()); // displays "Polygon"
```

This is the simplest way of adding a submodule to a main module but it does require the main module to be present in the scope, before we can add the submodule to it.

Adding submodules using asynchronous properties

Adding submodules to a hosting module using asynchronous properties has the advantage of being more flexible, in the sense that the hosting module does not need to be loaded before the submodule can be added to it.

Therefore, the submodule can potentially reside in a different file, and can be loaded and added to the hosting module at different times (either before or after the hosting module is loaded), in an asynchronous fashion.

Let's have a look at the following code snippet:

```
var Polygon_Module;

var Shape = (function(mainModule, subModule){

    var Polygon = mainModule.Polygon = mainModule.Polygon ||
subModule;

    Polygon.description = function(){

        return "submodule has been added to shape module";
```

```
    };

    return mainModule;

})(Shape || {}, Polygon_Module ||{});

console.log(Shape.Polygon.description());
```

This code is responsible for adding our submodule `Polygon_Module`, to our main module `Shape`.

As you can see, we are passing two parameters to our IIFE, one for the main module and the other for the submodule. When any of them does not yet exist in the execution context, we are passing an empty object to our IIFE.

Inside of the IIFE, we check to see if our `mainModule` has the property `Polygon`, which is in fact our submodule. If the property does exist, we just use it and add a new property to this submodule, called `description`.

If the property `Polygon` (the submodule) does not exist in our code execution context, we use the passed-in submodule and then add the new property `description` to it.

Let's check to see if we can access this new property on the submodule, as follows:

```
console.log(Shape.Polygon.description()); // displays "submodule has
been added to shape module"
```

Now, even if we add our `Shape` module (the hosting module) after our submodule to our execution context, we can still add our submodule to this module. We can also provide access to our submodule's properties, through the main (hosting) module.

Consider the code below:

```
var Shape = (function(module){

    var type = "Any 2D and 3D shape";

    module.getType= function(){
        return type;
    };

    return module;

})(Shape || {});
```

This implementation of our `Shape` module accepts one parameter, which can be either an empty object or a reference to an already existing `Shape` module. This means that, even if our `Shape` module was already created in our previous IIFE, which was responsible for adding our `Polygon_Module` to our `Shape` module, we are still able to re-define it.

To test this, we can run the following:

```
console.log(Shape.getType()); // displays "any 2D and 3D shape"

console.log(Shape.Polygon.description()); // displays "submodule has
been added to shape module"
```

The result confirms that we are able to access properties of the `Shape` module as well as our submodule, no matter which one is loaded first in our application.

You might also notice that the implementation above is very similar to our loose augmentation pattern that we discussed previously. The only real difference is that we are adding our submodule as a completely independent module to our main module, as opposed to just augmenting the main module with new properties.

Summary

In this chapter, we looked at a few more techniques which enable us to extend and modify our modules.

We considered how we can use various cloning approaches to create replicas of our modules and talked about the pros and cons of each approach. We also examined how we can use inheritance among modules so that a child module can utilize the functionality of its parent module as well as override its parent module's functionality, as needed.

In the last section of this chapter, we talked about submodules and looked at a couple of different techniques for adding submodules to our main (hosting) modules.

The next chapter will be more focused on the design of our application as a whole. We'll see how a flexible ecosystem can be created for our modules, which allows them to interact and work together, without being dependent on each other.

7
Base, Sandbox, and Core Modules

So far in this book, we have mostly looked at different techniques for creating and enhancing modules. However, our focus has been on the smaller pieces of the application.

In this chapter, we are going to take a holistic view of our application as a complete functioning body. We will see how its various pieces can be put together to create a robust and flexible ecosystem to deliver our ultimate goal, which is a working **Single-Page Application (SPA)**.

As you read through different sections of this chapter, keep in mind that all the pieces of the application are designed to work together in concert, while still adhering to the principles of maintainability and extensibility of a modular design.

In this chapter, we will cover:

- Base module and its design
- Sandbox and the principles behind sandboxing of our components
- Core and its related modules
- Components and how they are added to the application
- Plug-and-play, progressive enhancement, and graceful degradation in our application

Note that we will not get too deep into the coding aspect of things here, since I would really like you to focus on the architecture of the application, as opposed to being distracted with the details of the implementation. As such, there is no project code associated with this chapter of the book.

I should also mention that the architectural design concepts discussed in this chapter, and the next, are based on the design principles that I was originally introduced to by *Nicholas C. Zakas*, after watching one of his talks on the subject. He is one of my favorite authors and speakers. While our implementation will slightly deviate from his, the essence of our architecture will remain similar to his proposed architectural design.

Application architecture overview

To create a truly modular design for our application, we need to break it down into smaller functional pieces, in such a way that each piece will specialize in and be responsible for very specific tasks. This enables us to achieve the principle of separation of concerns and responsibilities.

The following diagram provides a depiction of our overall application design:

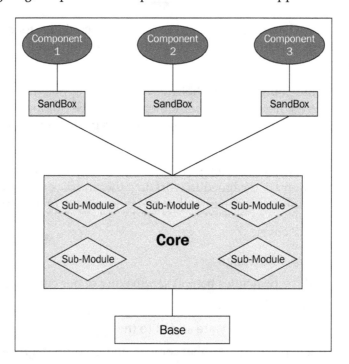

As you can see, our application consists of four main pieces:

- Base
- Sandbox
- Core
- Component

At the same time, each main piece may consist of other smaller pieces which are packaged together to create the main piece.

Let's start by exploring each main piece of the application and looking at the specific functionality that each piece provides.

For our purposes in this book, from this point forward, when I talk about **components**, I'll be referring to modules that have user interface pieces (views) which the user is able to interact with, such as the header component. However, when I refer to **modules** I will be referring to functional modules that each main piece may consist of, which do not have any views associated with them directly.

The definitions will become more clear as we move along but you may decide to refer to such pieces differently in your own projects. This is fine, as long as the architectural concepts behind them remain the same.

Also, from time to time, I will be referring to our modular design architecture as a **framework,** which should be interpreted as all the various pieces of the application together as a whole.

About the term framework

While I will be using the term framework at times, our application is not meant to create what is generally known as a framework. At least not in the same capacity that the term is used to refer to frameworks in the likes of **AngularJS** or **React**.

Generally speaking, I think sometimes third-party frameworks are overused and while they all provide some pros, there are also cons associated with using any type of third party framework.

The purpose of this book is to show you how you can create your own architectural design which allows you to easily create, organize, and maintain your application's code base without the need for a third party framework.

As such, I would like you to look at our implementation as an architectural design concept as opposed to a framework. But if you insist, you can call what we design and create here an **ironic framework**. I say ironic, because it is really not a framework in the traditional sense, as it does not impose a special syntax or a slew of rules and regulations!

The best way to describe our implementation is perhaps by using the term **Client-side Modular Design (CMD)**, since the goal of this architectural approach is to create a solid foundation and a flexible ecosystem for our applications, as opposed to it being a framework.

Base module

We will start our exploration of the design with the base module. As the name implies, the base module provides the lowest level of functionality for our application.

This is where we import and leverage the functionality of third party libraries and utilities. These libraries can consist of jQuery, Dojo, MooTools, and so on.

The main idea is that we can easily use the functionality provided by such libraries without the need to create a tight dependency between our application and the libraries used.

For instance, consider how we need to detect browser compatibility to attach events to our elements on the page, as follows:

```
if (elem.addEventListener) {
    elem.addEventListener(event, callbackFunc);
} else if (elem.attachEvent) { // For IE 8 and earlier versions
    elem.attachEvent("on" + event, callbackFunc);
}
```

Whereras we could easily let jQuery take care of such intricacies by doing the following:

```
$(elem).on(event,callbackFunc);
```

Here, we are letting jQuery take care of the browser compatibility issues and we can focus on other, more important things in our application. Another example is adding animations to our elements only when jQuery is present. This approach allows us to implement **progressive enhancement** and **graceful degradation** techniques in our code.

We can also have both of such implementations in our code. This allows us to have a fallback if jQuery has not been loaded properly.

Therefore, the preceding code can be written as follows:

```
if($) {
    $(elem).on(event,callbackFunc);

} else {
    if (elem.addEventListener) {
        elem.addEventListener(event, callbackFunc);
    } else  if (elem.attachEvent) {    // For IE 8
      and earlier versions
        elem.attachEvent("on" + event, callbackFunc);
    }
}
```

Most of the time, it is best to leave low-level functionality such as browser compatibility issues to third party libraries and focus on providing customized functionality for our application in our own code.

Keep in mind that we are talking about third party libraries and utility packages here and not third party frameworks, as one of the goals of our architecture is to eliminate, or at least minimize, the need for third party frameworks.

Adding general-purpose libraries to the base module

As mentioned, our base module loads and provides general-purpose libraries to the core module of our application. This means that only the core is aware of what base libraries are used in the code, as well as which particular functionality of such libraries is being leveraged.

Depending on the design of our base module, the libraries are either loaded at application start-up time or dynamically at a later time. The base module passes a reference for each loaded and initialized library to the core module.

Since it is only the core module that is aware of what libraries are used in the application and to what extend, if we ever decide to change our third party libraries or how they are used in the application, it is only the core module that is affected and no other pieces.

This means that all the other pieces and components of our application will continue to work as they did before, regardless of the change in the third party libraries. Implementing our application as such minimizes the impact of replacing or removing the third party libraries on the application as a whole.

This also holds true when we import and use new libraries in order to add more functionality to our application.

In the next chapter, we will have a closer look at how the base module is used to add jQuery to our application's core module.

The following is a depiction of how third party libraries are provided to the core module by our application's base module:

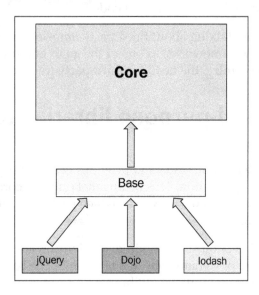

Sandbox module

When we talk about a sandbox in our daily lives, we usually have a picture of a box full of sand in our minds, where we allow the kids to play and make all the mess they like - and hopefully only in that box.

In our modular architecture, we capitalize on the same concept and create spaces for our components to play in and to be isolated from other pieces of the application.

By sandboxing our modules in such a way, we eliminate tight coupling among our application components and the core module.

The sandbox is essentially a layer of abstraction as well as a thin interface between our components and the other pieces of our application.

As the sandbox module is designed to be an interface and to provide communication among our components and the rest of the application, it is considered a contract and, as such, it should never change. This is so our components can be sure that they can always count on a consistent layer of communication with the application as well as a certain level of functionality provided by the core module.

That is not to say, we cannot add new methods or functionality to the sandbox; it is only that we cannot change what is already there and that our components have come to rely on.

Sandbox module functionality

When our components are loaded in the application, either at application start-up time or dynamically any time after, they are all given an instance of the sandbox module.

The sandbox module provides the following for our components:

- A consistent interface
- Security
- Communication
- Filtering

Each one of the services provided by the sandbox module is crucial to the modular aspect of our implementation.

Let's explore each aspect in more detail.

Sandbox as a consistent interface

As mentioned, when every registered component is given an instance of the sandbox module by the core module.

This instance of the sandbox then acts as an interface to the rest of the application, which provides application-level functionality for the component.

When a component needs a particular functionality, it does not necessarily need to implement it itself. This is true when the implementation of that functionality is already available in the application.

For instance, to bind event handlers to elements, each component does not need to provide its own implementation. Components can simply ask the sandbox module, which in turn, asks the core module to bind a certain event handler to a particular element on the page.

Of course, the components also do not have to worry about browser compatibility issues related to event binding, as it is the job of the core module to take care of such issues.

Since the sandbox instance is identical for every registered component, we can be sure that any changes in the sandbox code is provided to all the components at the same time. This means that the addition of new functionality, bug fixes, and modifications in the sandbox module are done once and then propagated to all the components that use the sandbox module, in a uniform and cohesive manner.

Note that any changes to the sandbox module should still honor the previous contract between this module and the application's components.

Sandbox as a security layer

The components in our application only know about the sandbox module and are not allowed (or able) to directly communicate with any other pieces of the application.

This means that the sandbox makes sure that protected areas of the framework are not accessible by the components through its interface. This enables us to control the type of operations that the components are permitted to perform, within the context of the core and other modules of the application.

Sandbox as a communication layer

As the sandbox module is a thin layer of interface which provides the exposed interface of the core module to the components, it is the only route of communication between the components and the rest of the application.

It is also through the sandbox module that components can subscribe to and publish custom events in the application.

Note that it is important for the components to only have one route of communication with the rest of the application so we can preserve the integrity of our modular design. If a component is able to directly communicate with another component or other parts of the application, then it could be tightly coupled to such pieces, and we certainly would like to avoid this type of tight coupling.

Sandbox as a filter

The design of the sandbox should be done in a way that not only will it provide the functionality of the core module that we want to expose to the components, but it can also do simple error checking for the calls made by the components to the core.

For instance, consider the following:

```
getElement : function(elementID){

    if(elementID && typeof elementID === "string"){
        return core.getElement(elementID);
    }else{
        core.log(3,"incorrect parameters passed
            in; from SandBox.getElement");
    }
}
```

The preceding method has been provided to our components through the sandbox module. This method does a simple parameter check to make sure that the parameter, as well as the correct type of the parameter, has been passed to it by the component before the sandbox module asks the core to do the work.

While the core module might have its own error checking, it is always a good idea to do some error checking at the sandbox level before getting the core module involved.

Implementing multiple instances of the sandbox module

You may be wondering at this point, why is it a better idea to use multiple instances of the sandbox module (one for each component) as opposed to having all the components use the same sandbox object as a singleton?

The short answer is: better isolation and performance. We need to explore that answer a little further in the upcoming sections.

Advantages of multiple instances of the sandbox

Usually, a module provides its exposed functionality to the outside world through a single common interface.

However, our implementation of the sandbox module is different. As mentioned previously, we create multiple instances of the sandbox module and, to be more precise, one instance per component.

The following summarizes the goals behind this design:

- Isolating sandbox instances from each other
- Creating a code execution context for each component
- Performance improvements

Isolating the sandbox instances from each other

In our analogy of a kid playing in a sandbox, I mentioned that this type of isolation contains the possible mess created in the box. In just the same way, we would like any possible damage to a sandbox module instance to be contained and isolated.

This would mean that, if one of our components does something undesirable which could cause issues in its sandbox instance, such a mess would be contained within that sandbox module instance. The adverse effects will only impact the functionality of that component but no other sandbox instances, or any other components for that matter.

It is very important for us to design our architecture in such a way which minimizes the chances of complete application failure caused by an issue in one of the components.

This allows for at least partial functionality of our application, which is probably a much more acceptable outcome than a complete application failure.

For instance, the footer component in our application may stop working but the user can still view the catalog of our images and add them to the favorites list.

Creating a code execution context

When a sandbox module is created, it sets a context object for its component. Components can use this context object to easily refer to the correct execution context when needed. This is probably better understood if we look at an example.

Consider the following code snippet from our application:

```
handleMainContainerClicked: function (e) {

    if (e.target != e.currentTarget) {

        e.preventDefault();
        e.stopPropagation();

        if (e.target.tagName.toUpperCase() === 'IMG') {
            sandBox.contextObj.handleImageClick(e.target);

        } else if (e.target.tagName.toUpperCase() === 'A') {
            sandBox.contextObj.handelFavLinkClick(e.target);
        }

    }
}
```

The function above is implemented in the content component of our application. Inside this function, which is the click event handler for some of the elements on the page, we need to call other related functions in the content component.

We can easily do that by using the execution context that we set on the sandbox instance for this component when we first initialize the component.

This is done as follows:

```
sandBox.contextObj = this;
```

In the code snippet, `this` refers to the content component of our application. Thus, when we need to execute any functions in the context of our content component, we can just refer to the correct context, as follows:

```
sandBox.contextObj.handelFavLinkClick(e.target);
```

If this does not make a lot of sense to you right now, do not be alarmed. I will explain this further in the next chapter where we'll have a chance to look at it's full implementation in the code.

For now, the only thing that you need to keep in mind is that we can use each instance of the sandbox module to preserve a reference to the component that the sandbox instance belongs to. This allows us to easily access the execution context of that component.

Performance improvements

When we create an instance of the sandbox for each component, we also assign a reference on the sandbox instance to the DOM element in which the component's view resides. This allows us to make our DOM manipulation within that container a lot more efficiently, since we do not need to traverse the whole DOM tree to find the DOM element of interest within the container of the component's view.

Have a look at the following code snippet:

```
getElementInContext : function(elementID){

    if(elementID && typeof elementID === "string"){
        return core.getChildOfParentByID(
            containerElemContext,elementID);

    }else{

        core.log(3,"incorrect parameters
            passed in; from SandBox.getElementInContext");
    }

}
```

In this snippet, we are trying to find a child element of the container element where the component's view has been rendered.

When the component was registered with the core, the core created an instance of the sandbox and returned a reference to the component's container element with the sandbox instance.

For instance, after the header component of our application is created, all the header-related DOM elements reside inside a main div element container that hosts them. The header component's sandbox instance holds a reference to this div container.

When the header component needs access to any DOM elements related to its view, it will only need to look for the desired element inside of its container div element as opposed to traversing the whole DOM tree to find the element.

This makes finding the desired element much quicker as we don't need to search the entire DOM looking for it.

If you are not completely clear on how this works, we will cover it again in the next chapter when we examine the code in more depth.

For now, just be mindful of the fact that the sandbox instance allows us to have quick and direct access to the DOM element that the component renders in, which in turn allows for much more optimized DOM manipulation tasks related to the component.

Core module

The core module is really the brain of our application. It is where the application's heavy lifting is done and the real magic happens.

The core module is responsible for implementing application-level business logic as well as providing bridges among components when there is a need for components to communicate with each other. Of course, while still preserving the loose coupling nature of the application.

The core module also leverages the functionality provided by the third party libraries, which are loaded by the base module, to create a cohesive functional application.

If you are familiar with the architectural design pattern known as **Module-View-Controller** (**MVC**), the core module is the controller piece of this design pattern in our application.

We can summarize the role of core module as the following:

- Acting as the controller for the application
- Providing communication bridges among modularized components
- Initializing and destroying components
- Implementing plug-and-play capability for the components
- Providing a centralized method of handling errors

- Providing application-level extensibility
- Leveraging third party libraries' functionality

We will examine all these aspects very shortly but before doing so, let's talk about how the core is constructed in our application.

Core module construction approach

There are different approaches to building the core module, but one of the best approaches is to build it in a modularized fashion.

We can start the implementation by building a main core module and then augment it using techniques such as loose and tight augmentation, which we have already covered in this book. However, adding most of the functionality to the core module using sub-modules allows for a better separation of the logic in the code.

In the implementation of our main application for this book, we will be using all the above techniques to build our core module.

The next chapter will examine the implementation of the core in depth, but for now, we'll look at a couple of things related to its implementation.

Consider the following:

```
var ImagesInc_Core = (function(Core){

    var $ = Core.jQuery;
    var insertHTMLTxt = function(containerID,newStructure){
        var containerElem;
        if(typeof containerID === 'string'){

            containerElem = Core.getElement(containerID);
        }else if(typeof containerID === 'object'){

            containerElem = containerID;
        }
        Core.setInnerHTML(containerElem,newStructure);
    };
    ...

    return Core;

})(ImagesInc_Core); // using tight augmentation
```

In the preceding code, we are using tight augmentation to add DOM-related functionality to the core module. We can also add functionality to the core by attaching a sub-module to it, as shown here:

```
// using simple sub-module augmentation
ImagesInc_Core.LoggingHandler = (function(){

    var self = {}, messageParam, colorParam;

    self.logMessage = function(severity, message,color) {
        // if no severity number was possed in,
          then give the message and warn the user
        if(typeof severity === 'string'){
            message = severity;
            severity = 2;
        }

    ...

    return {
            logMessage: self.logMessage,
            initialize: self.initialize
        };

})();
```

As you can see, we are augmenting the core module by attaching a self-contained sub-module, which is added as a new property to the core module object.

Augmenting the core module using sub-modules, is similar to building a play house using Lego blocks as separate pieces are attached together to create the whole structure.

This would mean that not only the application main pieces (such as components and sandbox) are built as modules, but also the core module itself is built based on smaller modules.

This allows us to easily extend our core module while providing us with the ability to remove or replace each sub-module without affecting the other pieces of the core module.

We will examine this modular implementation of the core module quite a bit further, when we'll have a look under the hood in the next chapter. Have a look at the following image to see all the pieces of the core module in our final application. This image depicts how the core module consists of separate self-contained sub-modules:

Of course, at the time of deployment, we can combine and minify all of these files (sub-modules) into one file but during development, this separation of sub-modules provides a good visual representation of all the pieces of the core module.

Now that we have had a good overview of how the core module is built, let's examine the functionality that this module provides for us.

Core module functionality

Core module plays different vital roles in our application, and provides essential services for all the other modules. It is important to note that while the core module consists of many pieces itself, it acts as a uniform and cohesive piece while providing the following functionality for the application.

Acting as the controller

The core module provides application-level functionality for all the components in the application. For instance, event binding and unbinding happen in the core module and the components only need to ask the core to take care of this task for them.

Consider the following code snippet:

```
if(elem.addEventListener) {
    elem.addEventListener(event, callbackFunc);
    } else if(elem.attachEvent) {
```

```
        // For IE 8 and earlier versions
            elem.attachEvent("on" + event, callbackFunc);
    }
}
```

This code is implemented in the core module and all the components in the application call this method (through their instance of the sandbox module) to bind an event handler to an element.

Another example can be when a component would need to make an **AJAX** call to the server. It is the core module that would make the call instead to the server and would return the result to the component and/or would take an action based on the result returned, such as logging an error when the AJAX call fails.

We can also mention **cookie** and **local storage**-related functionality in the application as some of the other application-level functionality the core provides to all the registered components.

Keep in mind that the implementation should be designed in a way that component-specific functionality that only the component cares about should happen at the component level and that the application-level functionality should take place at the core module.

Each component, in a sense, implements its own MVC or MV* design at the component level, which is separate from the application-level implementation. This point will become more clear to you when we look at implementation code in the next chapter.

Providing communication bridges

As you may recall, one of the main goals of our modular architecture was to provide loose coupling among our components. This means that none of the components in our application knows about any other component, nor are they dependent on any other component.

However, there are times when components need to communicate with each other, or an event or action in one component should cause a change in another component, while the components have no knowledge of each other.

To provide such functionality the core implements a variation to the observer pattern called the **mediator pattern**.

Using the mediator pattern, our application's components can register for and publish events. However, this is done through an abstraction layer.

The following is a depiction of how the mediator pattern is implemented:

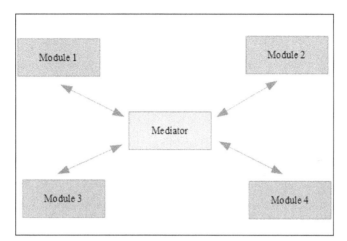

The core module in our application acts as the mediator, which enables the components (modules) for subscribe to and publish events without knowing about each other, thus still adhering to the principle of loose coupling among our components and modules.

Consider the following code snippet:

```
sandBox.publishCustomEvent({
        type: 'support-Clicked',
        data: "support"
});
```

Here, the footer component in our application is publishing a custom event, support-Clicked, through its instance of the sandbox module. Beyond that, it has no idea what other pieces of the application could be listening for this event and what actions they would take based on this event.

On the other hand, the following snippet shows that our NotificationHandler module is listening to this event and will take action when this event is published, as follows:

```
ImagesInc_Core.registerForCustomEvents("Notification",{
        'support-Clicked':this.handleSupportClick
}
```

The core module is responsible for notifying all the registered components and modules that a certain event has taken place if they have registered for that particular event.

Initializing and destroying components

In our architectural design, we can load and unload components (modules) both at the start-up phase of the application as well as any time after.

This is pretty robust, since it allows us to load what we need when we need it, which helps to keep the consumption of the resources on the device to a minimum, as well as keeping the application very light and responsive. This could be particularly important for mobile devices.

When a component is loaded (either at application start-up or any other time), it first registers itself with the core module and then the core module calls the `init` method of the component when it needs to be initialized.

Consider the following code snippet and see how this is done:

```
ImagesInc_Core.registerComponent("footerContainer",
  "footer", function(sandBox){

    return {

        init: function(){
            try{
                sandBox.updateElement("footerContainer",
                  ImagesInc_GlobalData.getFooterHTMLTxt());
                this.registerForEvents();
                sandBox.contextObj = this;
                sandBox.logMessage(1,'Footer component
                  has been initialized...', 'blue');

            }catch(e){
                sandBox.logMessage(3,'Footer component has NOT
                  been initialized correctly --> ' + e.message);
            }
        },
```

As you can see in the preceding code, each component upon loading calls the `registerComponent` method of the core module. Note that the core module is known as `ImagesInc_Core` to other application pieces.

The component sends the ID of its container (`footerContainer` for instance) as well as its own ID (shown as `footer` in the preceding code) as parameters to the `registerComponent` method of the core module.

It also sends a reference to the function that the core module needs to call to create an instance of the component. This function is then called by the core module with an instance of the sandbox module, which is an interface for the component to use for interacting with the application from this point forward.

Here is how registration of the component is done in the core module:

```
mainCore.registerComponent = function(containerID,
  componentID, createFunc){
...
if(createFunc && typeof createFunc === 'function'){
    componentObj = createFunc(new
      SandBox(this,containerElem, componentID));
    if (componentObj.init && typeof componentObj.init ===
    'function' && componentObj.destroy && typeof
    componentObj.destroy === 'function') {

        componentObj.id = componentID;
        registeredComponents.push(componentObj);
    }
...
};
```

As you can see, the core module first checks to see if the component has the required methods, `init` and `destroy`, and if so, the creator function (`createFunc`) on the component is called to create an instance of the component.

You can think of this phase as the hand-shake phase between the component and the core module specifically, as well as the hand-shake of the component with the application as a whole.

As mentioned, the component is also required to have a destroy method, which allows the core module to either disable the component for event handling and/or to completely remove the component from the application.

At the start-up phase of application, the core module goes through all the registered components and calls the `init` method on all of them, as shown:

```
for(var i=0; i < registeredComponents.length; i++){

  registeredComponents[i].init();
}
```

We use a similar approach to destroy (remove) all the registered components from the application, as shown:

```
for(var i=lastIndex; i >= 0 ; i--){

    registeredComponents[i].destroy(removeFromDom);
}
```

We will look at the details of these operations in the next chapter and will examine the code more closely then. The takeaway here is that the core module handles the initialization and destruction of all the components in the application, either as a collection or on individual basis.

Providing plug-and-play capability

As we mentioned previously, components can be loaded and added to the application at any time while the application is loaded in the browser.

Let's have a look at how a component is loaded dynamically and how it becomes part of the application.

Dynamic loading of the components is done by leveraging a mechanism which first checks to see if the component is already loaded in the cache, and if not, finding its object definition in either the local storage or in the `PageDefinitions.js` file and then subsequently loading it.

The `PageDefinitions.js` is the file that holds object definitions (as JavaScript objects) for all the components that can be loaded dynamically in the application, at any time other than the start-up phase.

We can also keep resource (asset) information related to any component in this file if we desire to do so. Generally speaking, this file is mostly used to find the location of our dynamic assets.

For instance, in our application, we will be keeping information related to the `Favorites` page and the location of its CSS file in `PageDefinitions.js`. This information will be consumed by the content component when the user navigates to this page.

Have a look at the following diagram to see an overview of the dynamic component-loading mechanism in our application:

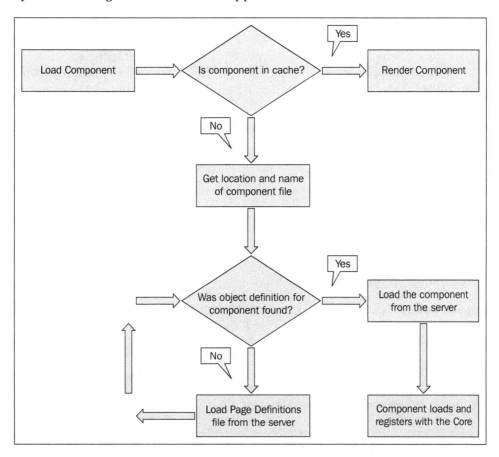

As the flow diagram shows, when there is a need for a component to be rendered dynamically in the application, the core module checks to see if the component object is already present in the cache.

If the component object is already present in the cache, then there is no need to do anything else but to render its view.

On the other hand, if the component object is not present, the core module looks for the component's object definition in the local storage first. This object definition has a property that holds the location (path) of the component's JavaScript file on the server.

Note that we are using the local storage as the primary storage facility for such object definitions as opposed to keeping them in the cache. This is purely to keep the footprint of the application as small as possible in the browser. Usage of the local storage is especially important if we have quite a few object definitions for the components, since such, definitions could get quite large and consume a considerable amount of memory.

Admittedly, in our application there is no real need to use local storage, since we have only one dynamically loading component. But I'm using the local storage to show you how it can be leveraged if you decide to use this mechanism in your future applications.

The important point is that when the core finds the location of the component's file, it will make a request to the server for the .js (and possibly .css) file(s) of the component.

Once the required .js file for the component is loaded and parsed, then the component registers itself with the core and, as with any other component in the application, it is given an instance of the sandbox module.

As you can imagine, this approach provides us with a very robust way to dynamically load and activate our application's components, which essentially encompasses the plug-and-play capabilities of the application.

The mechanism is a bit more involved than what is explained here, but this brief description should provide a good overview of how things work behind the scenes. In the next chapter, we will have a closer look at the implementation of this mechanism and I'm sure all the details will become more clear to you in that chapter.

Providing a centralized approach to handling errors

The core module implements a centralized approach to logging all types of messages. This frees the application modules and components from implementing such functionality themselves. It also provides enhanced capabilities for the logging mechanism that all components can leverage in a uniform way.

Note that any future enhancements that we may make to our logging mechanism will be done in one place and will be available to all the modules at the same time.

For instance, imagine that we would like all the error messages in the application to be logged on the server. This could mean that for each error, an AJAX call needs to be made from the client to the server with the related information.

If each module wanted to do that task itself, we would have to implement such functionality for each module separately. Of course, it makes more sense to implement this functionality once and then provide it to all of the application modules in a cohesive manner.

Have a look at the following screenshot, which displays our application messages being logged in the Chrome debugger tool when the application is in the debug mode:

```
Core Module has been initialized...                              MainCore.js:25
LoggingHandler Module has been initialized...                    Logger.js:27
Utilities Module has been initialized...                         Logger.js:27
CookieHandler Module has been initialized...                     Logger.js:27
LocalStorage is availble.                                        Logger.js:27
StorageHandler Module has been initialized...                    Logger.js:27
AjaxEngine Module has been initialized...                        Logger.js:27
NotificationHandler Module has been initialized...               Logger.js:27
Initializing all components...                                   Logger.js:27
Core is listening to custom events now...                        Logger.js:27
Header component has been initialized...                         Logger.js:27
Footer component has been initialized...                         Logger.js:27
Content component has been initialized...                        Logger.js:27
NotificationHandler is listening to custom events now...         Logger.js:27
All components have been initialized...                          Logger.js:27
Page has changed /index.html                                     Logger.js:29
```

As you can see, when the application is loaded, all the modules as well as all the components in the application are initialized and the related messages are displayed.

All that the components need to do is call the sandbox module with the message, and the sandbox module in turn will send the message to the core module. In the case of other core modules, they can directly use the core module's logging mechanism.

Here is a code snippet which shows how the footer component logs its initialization message using the core module's logging mechanism:

```
sandBox.logMessage(1,'Footer component has
   been initialized...', 'blue');
```

To log an error message, the footer component only needs to do the following:

```
sandBox.logMessage(3,'Footer component has NOT been initialized
correctly --> ' + e.message);
```

This is a much simpler and better approach than the footer component implementing its own error-handling mechanism.

If we decide to send all the error messages to the server, the module, will still make the same call to the sandbox module and in turn to the core module. It will be the core module that will be responsible for sending the error message to the server.

The following code snippet shows how one of the core sub-modules sends its initialization message to the core module. This is similar to how the components log their message but with one difference.

```
ImagesInc_Core.log(1,"Utilities Module has
    been initialized...", "blue");
```

The difference is that the sub-module directly sends its message to the core module and not through a sandbox module instance. This is, of course, because the sub-module is part of the core module and does not have an instance of the sandbox module.

Also, the sandbox module itself uses the same logging facility provided by the core module to log its errors, as shown:

```
Core.log(3,"incorrect parameters passed in; from
    SandBox.getElement ");
```

The following image shows how the error message is displayed in the debugger:

```
Header component has been initialized...                                         Logger.js:27
⊘ ► incorrect parameters passed in; from SandBox.addEventHandlerToElement        Logger.js:29
Footer component has been initialized...                                         Logger.js:27
```

We will have a more in-depth look at how the logging mechanism has been implemented in our application, and how it is designed to be a sub-module of the core module, in the next chapter.

Providing application-level extensibility

From the beginning, we designed our application based on modular architecture. One of the advantages that our modular architecture provides is the ability to easily extend our application's functionality and capabilities when needed.

As you saw, the functionality of our application was enhanced using various techniques, such as loose augmentation, tight augmentation, and sub-modules.

While our application might provide quite a bit of functionality, it is a reasonable to assume that more features and capabilities will be needed in the future.

For instance, imagine that one or more of our future components need to do form field validation. This functionality can be easily added to our application by extending the core module and then providing the functionality to our components.

The core module can provide form field validation by either importing a validation library through the base module or by implementing the functionality itself. This new functionality will then be provided to all the registered components through the sandbox module and all the components can use it as needed.

In fact, our components would not even know who has provided this new functionality and how it works behind the scenes. All they need to know is that the functionality is available to them and they can use it to accomplish their validation tasks.

Being able to provide application-level extensibility is one of the key features of our modular design and one of the most important tasks that the core module is responsible for.

Leveraging third party libraries

We briefly talked about this responsibility of the core module before. As mentioned, the core module is designed to ask for third party libraries from the base module. These libraries are used by the core module to provide application-level functionality for other pieces of the application.

The import of such libraries usually happens at the application start-up time, but it does not have to.

As you saw previously in this chapter, our application does have the capability to load files dynamically from the server. It is quite possible that while the application is running, based on certain application needs or certain user interactions with the application, we need to load a third party library dynamically.

Most of the time, we would use the dynamic loading of a third party library when the library is not needed for most of the functionality of our application. This allows us to keep the foot print of our application small, which is an important consideration on mobile devices.

In the application for this book, we do not use such dynamic loading of third party libraries. However, if at any point in the future you decide to leverage this capability, all the hooks are available for it in the code.

Let's have a look at how the core module uses the base module to import the jQuery library into our application.

Consider the following:

```
(function Core_initialize(){

        mainCore.debug = true;
```

```
try{
    // get jQuery from the base module loader
    mainCore.jQuery = $ = ImagesInc_Base.getBaseModule();

}catch(e){

    if(mainCore.debug){
        console.error('Base Module has
            not been defined!!!' );
    };
};

if(mainCore.debug){
    console.log("%c Core Module has been initialized...",
"color:blue");
    };

})();
```

In the preceding code snippet, during the start-up phase of the application, our core module (`MainCore` module of the core module) asks the base module for jQuery.

This is done as shown here:

```
mainCore.jQuery = $ = ImagesInc_Base.getBaseModule();
```

Notice that we have wrapped this call in a try/catch statement to capture any errors that could happen during this operation.

Let's also have a look at how the base module provides a reference for jQuery to the core module.

```
if(typeof jQuery !== 'undefined'){
    return jQuery;
}else{
    return null;
}
```

As you can see, since jQuery loads as a global object in the application, the base module simply returns a reference to this global object to the core module. From that point forward, jQuery is used by the core module as a sub-module to deliver application-level functionality.

The following code snippet shows an example of how jQuery is used in the application to provide the required functionality:

```
var ImagesInc_Core = (function(Core){
    var $ = Core.jQuery;
    Core.makeAjaxCall = function(url, theQuery, method, handler){

        if($ && Core.jQueryAjaxEngine &&
          Core.jQueryAjaxEngine.makeAjaxCall){
            Core.jQueryAjaxEngine.makeAjaxCall(url,
              theQuery, method, handler);

        }else{
            Core.log(3, "Cannot make Ajax call!; from
              makeAjaxCall")
        }
    };
    ...
})(ImagesInc_Core); // using tight augmentation
```

Just in the same way, other third party libraries can be loaded into the application at the start-up phase to enhance our application's functionality.

Note that none of the other modules or components are aware of the third party libraries or how they are leveraged. It is only the core module that is aware of such libraries, and it is the only module to provide the third party library functionality to other application modules and components.

The following image shows how third party libraries can be placed in our application's folder structure:

Components

The last main piece of our application design is related to components. In this section, we will cover how components are built and plugged into our application.

Remember that we considered components as pieces of the application that have views. By views, I am referring to the pieces that have HTML elements associated with them which are rendered in the browser and the users can interact with them directly.

Components can be as simple as a layover box. Such simple components can be rendered as part of another component or as a stand-alone component on their own.

Most of the time, our components are independent modules with their own MVC or MV* architecture, which are attached to the application and use the facilities and functionality that the rest of the application provides for them.

In our design, we have created three main components and a widget named `NotificationWidget`. This widget is also a component but it is loaded and viewed based on the user's interaction with another component. In our application, `NotificationWidget` is launched when the user clicks on the **Support** link in the footer component. Since this widget can potentially be launched by other components too, I am tagging it as a widget but for all practical intents and purposes, it is also a component with its own MV* implementation.

Components can have very sophisticated business logic implemented in their controller, or have a very simple controller with very little functionality.

In our application, the content component is an example of a component with a fairly involved controller logic, and the footer stands as a component with a relatively simple controller.

Also remember that the only bridge or point of connection between a component and the rest of the application is via an instance of the sandbox which was passed to it when the component registered itself with the core.

We previously talked about how, in our architecture, components can be loaded either at the start-up phase of the application or dynamically at any time after that. In our implementation, header, footer, and the content components are loaded at the start-up phase and `NotificationWidget` is loaded dynamically, when required.

Let's have a look at one of our simpler components, the footer, and see how it is implemented.

Components required methods

In our design, there are two required methods that every component needs to implement in order to register and connect with the core module and the rest of the application.

These two required methods are called `init` and the `destroy` methods. The `init` method is called by the core module to start the initialization of the component. On the other hand, the `destroy` method is called by the core module to either disable or completely remove the component from the application.

Consider the implementation below:

```
init: function(){
        try{
            sandBox.updateElement("footerContainer",
                ImagesInc_GlobalData.getFooterHTMLTxt());
            this.registerForEvents();
            sandBox.contextObj = this;
            sandBox.logMessage(1,'Footer component has
                been initialized...', 'blue');

        }catch(e){
            sandBox.logMessage(3,'Footer component has NOT
                been initialized correctly --> ' + e.message);
        }
},

    destroy: function(removeComponent){

        sandBox.contextObj.unregisterFromEvents();
        sandBox.unregisterAllCustomEvents();

        if(removeComponent){
            sandBox.removeComponent("footerContainer");
        }
        sandBox.logMessage(1,'Footer component has been
            destroyed...', "blue");
    }
```

As you can see, in the `init` method of the footer component, the required HTML string for the view is fetched from the `GlobalData` object. This object is an application-level object (the application model) which holds application-level data. The HTML string is then passed to the core module via the sandbox module instance.

Note that the core module is responsible for rendering HTML elements, in this case the footer's view, on the page.

This is done in the following lines of code in the `init` method:

```
sandBox.updateElement("footerContainer", ImagesInc_GlobalData.
getFooterHTMLTxt());
```

For this particular component, we call for the rendering of the view in this method. However, the rendering does not always have to be done in the `init` method of a component. For instance, for `NotificationWidget` component, the rendering is done in a different method which is called at some later time by the application. Consequently, the `init` method of `NotificationWidget` is kept very simple, as follows:

```
init: function(){
            try{
                sandBox.contextObj = this;
                sandBox.logMessage(1,'Notification Widget component
has been initialized...', 'blue');

            }catch(e){
                sandBox.logMessage(3,'Notification Widget has NOT been
initialized correctly --> ' + e.message);
            }
    }
```

Binding events to the components elements

In `init` method of the footer component, we also register the HTML elements related to its view for handling events. This is done by calling `registerForEvents` method of the component. In `registerForEvents` method, the related event handler is bound to the `support` link, as follows:

```
registerForEvents : function(){
            .....................
            sandBox.addEventHandlerToElement("support","click", this.
handleSupportClick);

    }
```

As you can see, the actual binding for the event is done in the core module.

I previously mentioned that our components are loosely coupled with the other pieces of the application by custom events using the mediator pattern. Let's have a quick look at that.

Consider the following code snippet:

```
handleSupportClick : function(e){

        sandBox.publishCustomEvent({
            type: 'support-Clicked',
            data: "support"
        });

        e.preventDefault();
        e.stopPropagation();
}
```

As you can see, the footer component publishes a custom event when the **Support** link is clicked. Then, all the other pieces of the application that have registered for this custom event will be notified by the core module that this event has occurred. We will talk about this mechanism more in the next chapter.

Component design considerations

In this chapter, we did not examine the implementation details of the components too closely, as we will have a more in-depth look at them in the next chapter. However, I would like you to consider a few conceptual aspects of the components.

First of all, all the components are loosely coupled with the application. The only connection between them and the rest of the application is through an instance of the Sandbox, which was passed to them during the registration phase.

Second, all the components are responsible for implementing their own controllers. The other application pieces do not get involved with the functionality, which is specific to an individual component.

The job of the application as a whole, and the core module in particular, is to create a robust ecosystem in which the components can leverage the application-level functionality that has been implemented. Therefore, the components do not need to implement such functionality themselves. This approach allows us to create a cohesive and loosely coupled application that can be easily maintained and extended as the need arises.

Note that each Component is a self-contained piece of the application and the core or any other pieces of the application are not aware of nor are dependent on the internal implementation of the Component. This means that components are free to decide on their own implementation.

In this manner, we can create a good level of separation of concerns and responsibilities throughout all the application pieces.

When a component needs to modify the DOM, it should do so by leveraging the functionality that the core module provides. Therefore the component does not have to implement this functionality itself. Also, by using the core module, we are able to prevent other pieces of the application from accidentally causing any conflicts at the same DOM element level, thus preventing collisions and application-level issues.

The proper approach in most cases is that components only modify the DOM elements (through the core module) in their own container and not beyond that.

Application architectural considerations

Let's review the important points that we have discussed about our modular architecture in this chapter and see how they relate to various pieces of our application, as follows:

- All third party libraries are imported into the application through the base module

- The core module and the base module are the only pieces of the application that know about the loaded third party libraries

- All browser compatibility issues are dealt with in the core module by leveraging the functionality of the third party libraries

- Every component in the application gets an instance of the sandbox module

- The sandbox only knows about the core and no other pieces of the application

- No pieces of the application know about the internal implementation of other pieces

- Components can be added, modified, or removed from the application without affecting the application as a whole

- Components can only call their own methods and the methods provided to them through their instance of the sandbox module

- Components cannot access DOM elements outside of their own container
- Components should not create global objects
- Each module and component only does limited tasks and only things which are directly related to its own functionality
- All the components in the application are loosely coupled with the rest of the application
- Components can only communicate with other components and other pieces of the application using a publish-subscribe model (the mediator pattern) and their sandbox instance, thus preserving the loose coupling architecture
- Each component has a very limited understanding of the application, and that is through the instance of the sandbox module which was assigned to it during the registration phase of the component with the application

The following can be considered as the advantages that modular architecture provides for us:

- Once the modular architecture ecosystem has been developed, it can be used for many applications; therefore, we can code once and use many times
- Each piece of the application can be tested separately
- Each piece of the application can be implemented by different people in a modularized fashion
- Third party external dependencies can be controlled and managed by the core module
- Modules and components can be replaced, modified, or removed without affecting the application as a whole
- Components and modules can be loaded dynamically and as needed after the application start-up phase

I hope you view the points above as important takeaways from this chapter and will keep them in mind as we move forward to a more in-depth look at the application's implementation in the next chapter.

Summary

As was noted in the beginning of this chapter, we had a good overview of the architectural concepts related to the modular implementation of our application.

We discussed the main pieces of the application and saw how they come together to create a cohesive ecosystem.

We also examined the specific roles that the pieces play in the overall application design and looked at how we can create a good separation of responsibilities and concerns among our modules and components.

One of the important aspects that we focused on was to loosely couple our various application pieces together, which allows for ease of maintainability as well as future extensibility.

While some application code was shown in the chapter, we did not get deeply involved in analyzing the code and the application implementation. This is exactly what we will cover in the next chapter, where we will have a closer look at how things are done under the hood.

8

Application Implementation – Putting It All Together

After discussing the architectural concepts of our modular design in the previous chapter, it is time for us to look at the actual implementation.

The goal of this chapter is to examine the code and see how all the pieces fit and work together in a real application.

While we will not discuss every aspect of the code, each main piece will be broken down into smaller pieces, and most of the details will be explained.

I highly recommend that you download the project code related to this chapter from the site accompanying this book and follow along as we go through the finer points of the code. I am using different techniques at different parts of the code, which at first glance, might look inconsistent. However, this is done intentionally so that you can see how different techniques can be applied as needed, in different contexts.

Also, keep in mind that many aspects of the application can be improved upon as the focus has been on creating a **Proof Of Concept** (**POC**) application as opposed to production quality code. You will see how our modular approach allows us to create an easily maintainable, extensible, and robust application.

In this chapter, we will:

- Look at the main modules in the application
- Examine how components in the application have been constructed
- Discuss the overall architecture of the application
- Look at our publish-subscribe implementation, which provides loose coupling among our modules and components
- Implement a simple client-side router

But before examining the implementation, let's have a look at the final view of our application.

The user's view of our application

If you load index.html file of our project using an IDE which has a built-in web server, you will see the following main page in the browser. This file resides at the root of the application folder.

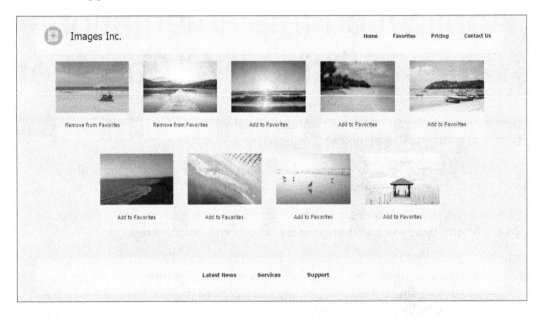

As you may have noticed, I have made improvements to the look and feel of the application, in comparison to what we had in the previous chapters. I have also done some re-factoring of the code in the project.

I mentioned previously that our application is somewhat responsive based on the browser's view-port. The following screenshot shows the application's `index.html` page in the Chrome Developer Tools emulator (*Ctrl* + *Shift* + *M* in Windows), simulating its rendering in an Apple iPad:

Application functionality

As you may recall, our application was intended to be an image gallery-type application which displays a list of images. Users are able to interact with the application in a variety of different ways. While the application might seem very simple from a user's point of view, it is designed from the ground up, to be easily extensible, so more functionality can be added to it as needed.

Let's consider the various aspects of our application's functionality.

Index page

The main page of the application (`index.html`) consists of three main components: `header`, `footer`, and `content`.

These components build the header, footer, and content sections (page fragments) of the main page respectively, as shown in the previous screenshot.

Since we designed our application as a **Single Page Application** (**SPA**), navigation to different pages of the application only updates the view of the content area.

The footer and header sections of the application are rendered only once, and that is at the initial load time of `index.html`. The main advantage of our SPA design is that there is no need to fully re-render the page every time different pages are viewed. Therefore, there is no flickering of the page in the browser.

In the main page, users are able to see the full catalog of all the images available. By clicking on an image, the user can see its full-size. Images can also be added to, or removed from, the list of favorite images when the user clicks on the related link below each image.

Users are able to interact with the header and footer of the application too, even though, for our POC, not all the links in the footer and header are activated.

Image page

When a user clicks on an image, the view of the content area of the application is changed to show the image in full view, as shown:

If you look at the address bar of the browser, the URL of the page changes when an image is clicked to reflect the ID of the image. For the preceding image, the URL of the page will be similar to:

```
http://127.0.0.1:49202/Image_9.jpg
```

This is the URL of your local server along with the image ID.

Favorites page

In the main page of our application, a user can click on the link at the bottom of each image to add the image to the list of his/her favorite images, as shown:

Once **Add to Favorites** link has been clicked, the text of the link changes to **Remove from Favorites**, which enables the user to remove the image from the list of favorite images.

Users can also view all of their favorite images by clicking the **Favorites** link in the header section of the page; which takes the user to the **Favorites** page of the application, as displayed:

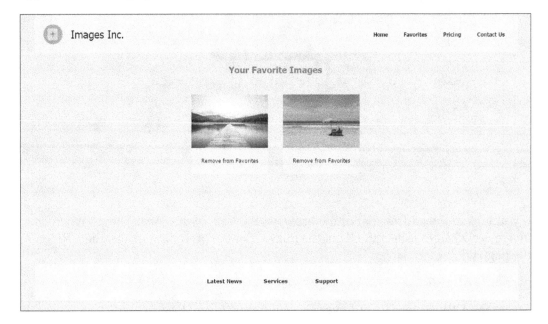

Support widget

When a user clicks on the **Support** link in the footer section of the application, a dialog box will be displayed with information regarding the site's catalog.

This widget (the dialogue box) has been designed to be dynamically loaded, and rendered on the page, but only when the **Support** link is clicked. This is an example of how components can be loaded and rendered dynamically in the application, as needed. This allows us to keep the weight of the application in the browser light and minimize its footprint.

The design of this widget also demonstrates the concept of plug-and-play in respect to dynamic components in the application.

The following screenshot shows how this widget is displayed in the browser:

Now that we have had a look at the appearance of the application, it is time to examine the mechanics of its implementation and see how things are done under-the-hood.

Application implementation

From the beginning, our intent in the design of our application was to create a modularized ecosystem in which different pieces of the code (modules) would be joined together to create a fully functional application. To that end, our code has been structured as displayed in the following screenshot:

As you can see, our application has been organized into three main folders: css which hosts all of our styling files, Images which stores all the images in the application's catalog; and js, which contains all the JavaScript code for our application. As this structure is only one approach to organizing the application's code, you may decide to organize the code differently.

Under js folder, we have organized our JavaScript files further into three main sub-folders; Components which contains the files related to modules that have views associated with them, Modules which contains our modules for the controller and Model of the application, and Widgets which hosts files related to components that are loaded and rendered dynamically in our application.

Our Modules folder is further broken down into five sub-folders; Base which contains our third-party dependencies and the base module, Core which hosts the controller's code (modules) for our application, and GlobalData which holds our application's model files.

The other two sub-folders, SandBox and PageDefinitions contain the sandbox module and object definitions file for our dynamically loading components, respectively.

We will examine the code in most of the files of our sub-folders in the following sections.

Loading our module files in index.html

Before we start looking at our JavaScript code and modules, let's have a closer look at index.html file and see how the application modules are loaded in the browser.

Our index.html page is designed in such a way that it only provides the bare minimum skeleton for our application's main page, and all the other pieces (header, footer, and content) are built dynamically when the page is loaded.

Generally speaking, there are instances when it makes more sense to build some of the pieces of the application's pages on the server before sending them to the client, since this implementation could provide better performance at times.

In our approach here, we are building all the pieces of our application's pages on the client. This is so we can examine and apply different concepts of our application's design a little easier.

The skeleton of our index.html file consists of three main containers, as follows:

```
<header id="headerContainer" role="banner" itemscope
  itemtype="https://schema.org/WPHeader"
  class="headerContainerClass">
</header>

<main id="mainPageContainer" role="main" class="clearfix
  mainPageContainerClass">
</main>

<div id="footerParentContainer" class="footerContainerClass" >
    <div id="footerContainer"
      class="footerlinksContainerClass">
    </div>
</div>
```

As you can see, we have our header container, which hosts the header component of our application, the main container, which hosts the content component of our application and a div, which is the container for our footer component.

These are the pieces (containers) in our `index.html` page which are passed to our components so they can render themselves inside of them.

Just before the closing tag for the page's body element, we have included the `<script>` tags which load the scripts for our application. Let's have a look:

```
<!--loading base and GlobalData modules-->
<script type="text/javascript"    src="js/Modules/Base/Base.js" ></script>
<script type="text/javascript"    src="js/Modules/Base/jquery-1.10.2.min.js" ></script>
<script type="text/javascript"    src="js/Modules/GlobalData/GlobalData_Sub.js" ></script>
<script type="text/javascript"    src="js/Modules/GlobalData/GlobalData.js" ></script>

<!--loading app core modules-->
<script type="text/javascript"    src="js/Modules/Core/MainCore.js" ></script>
<script type="text/javascript"    src="js/Modules/Core/Logger.js" ></script>
<script type="text/javascript"    src="js/Modules/Core/Utilities.js" ></script>
<script type="text/javascript"    src="js/Modules/Core/CookieHandler.js" ></script>
<script type="text/javascript"    src="js/Modules/Core/StorageHandler.js" ></script>
<script type="text/javascript"    src="js/Modules/Core/AjaxEngine.js" ></script>
<script type="text/javascript"    src="js/Modules/Core/NotificationHandler.js" ></script>
<script type="text/javascript"    src="js/Modules/SandBox/SandBox.js" ></script>

<!--loading app components-->
<script type="text/javascript"    src="js/Components/ImagesInc_Header.js" ></script>
<script type="text/javascript"    src="js/Components/ImagesInc_Footer.js" ></script>
<script type="text/javascript"    src="js/Components/ImagesInc_Content.js" ></script>
```

As you can see, quite a few script files need to be loaded. We can improve on this by combining (and minifying) some of the files together, as well as using formats such as **Asynchronous Module Definition** (**AMD**) in conjunction with libraries like `Require.js` to load our files. For now however, for the sake of clarity, we leave things as they are.

In *Chapter 10, Enterprise Grade Modular Design, AMD, CommonJS, and ES6 Modules* of this book, we will discuss how we can use AMD format to combine and load our application's required files in a more optimized way.

The following script has also been implemented in our `index.html` file, which is responsible for starting up the application.

```
<script type="text/javascript">

    ImagesInc_Core.initializeAllModules();
    ImagesInc_Core.initializeAllComponents();
    ImagesInc_Core.handlePageChange(location.pathname);

</script>
```

We will discuss how the start-up of the application takes place shortly. Notice that we initialize all the modules first, then the components, and at the end, we pass the URL of the page to `handlePageChange` method of `ImagesInc_Core` module. This is done, so we can use the URL of the page in our application's router, which will be examined in depth shortly.

I emphasize the point that as you are reading this chapter, you should probably load the related code into your IDE so you can easily follow along.

Base module implementation

Let's start the exploration of our application's modules with the base module. Our `Base` folder hosts two JavaScript files; `Base.js` and `jquery-1.10.2.min.js`.

`Base.js` file implements `ImagesInc_Base` module which is responsible for importing all of our third-party libraries into the application, as we discussed in the previous chapter. Currently, the only third-party library that we are importing is jQuery.

The following code snippet shows how this is implemented:

```
var ImagesInc_Base = (function(){
    function getBaseModule(){
        if(typeof  jQuery !== 'undefined'){
            return jQuery;
        }else{
            return null;
        }
    }
    return {
      getBaseModule: getBaseModule
    };
})();
```

As you can see, we are using an IIFE to return an object to the global variable `ImagesInc_Base`.

In this function, we first check to see if a jQuery object has been defined in the global scope; if so, we return it. Otherwise, `null` is returned.

Our core module will be using this object to leverage the jQuery library's functionality.

This is done in `MainCore` module as follows:

```
(function Core_initialize(){
        mainCore.debug = true;
        try{
            // get jQuery from the base module loader
            mainCore.jQuery = $ = ImagesInc_Base.getBaseModule();
        }catch(e){
            if(mainCore.debug){
                console.error('Base Module has not been
                defined!!!' );
            }
        }
        if(mainCore.debug){
            console.log("%c Core Module has been
            initialized...", "color:blue");
        }

})();
```

As our `MainCore` module is initializing itself (using an IIFE), it asks the base module for its base library and then assigns a reference of the returned object in both the `$` and `mainCore.jQuery` properties of `MainCore` module.

Note that in the current implementation, we are only able to import one base library. This is to keep the implementation simple, as we only need jQuery in our application. However, we could also import and use a collection of libraries with some modification to this code.

Core module implementation

The Core module is the heavy-lifter module in our application, and is constructed using a few sub-modules. This module's functionality has also been enhanced and augmented using the techniques that we discussed in the previous chapters, such as tight and loose augmentation.

Here is a list of all the sub-modules that make up the Core module:

We will not cover all the related code for this module but we will have a look at the important parts of it in this section. Note that the Core module is also the controller of our application.

MainCore module implementation

This module provides the main functionality of the Core module and all the related Core's sub-modules are attached to this module, hence the name `MainCore.js`.

I'll be referring to this module as **MainCore** from this point forward.

This module has been defined as follows:

```
var ImagesInc_Core = (function(mainCore){
var $ = null, registeredModules = [], registeredComponents = []....
...
...

})(ImagesInc_Core || {}); // using loose augmentation
```

As you can see, we have used the loose augmentation technique in this module to enhance its functionality.

This module also uses an inner IIFE to initialize itself and to import our application's base library. When the application is in debug mode, MainCore will announce that it has been initialized as soon as it is loaded.

This is shown in the following code snippet:

```
(function Core_initialize(){
        mainCore.debug = true;
        try{
            // get jQuery from the base module loader
            mainCore.jQuery = $ = ImagesInc_Base.getBaseModule();

        }catch(e){
            if(mainCore.debug){
                console.error('Base Module has
                    not been defined!!!' );
            }
        }
        if(mainCore.debug){
            console.log("%c Core Module has been
                initialized...", "color:blue");
        }
})();
```

To turn the debug mode on or off in the application, we have implemented the following method which can be called by the external code:

```
mainCore.toggleDebug = function(){
        mainCore.debug = !mainCore.debug;
        if(mainCore.debug){
            mainCore.log(1, "Application debug has
            been turned on...", "blue");
        }else{
            console.log("%c Application debug has been
            turned off...", "color:orange");
        }
};
```

Notice that we are returning a reference to MainCore module as a global variable, ImagesInc_Core, which allows the external code to interact with this module, through the interface that this module provides.

Augmenting MainCore module

In designing MainCore module, I have purposely used various augmentation techniques. This is done to demonstrate the practical aspects of such techniques in enchaining modules.

Augmenting MainCore using tight augmentation

Consider the following augmentation:

```
// event related functionality augmentation
var ImagesInc_Core = (function(Core){
    var $ = Core.jQuery;
    var addEventHandlerToElem = function(elem,event,callbackFunc){

        if(!elem){
            Core.log(3, 'elem is not passed in,
            from addEventHandlerToElem');
            throw new Error('Element not found');
        }
...

    Core.addEventHandlerToElement = addEventHandlerToElem;
    Core.removeEventHandlerFromElem = removeEventHandlerFromElem;
    Core.registerForCustomEvents = registerForCustomEvents;
............
    return Core;
})(ImagesInc_Core); // using tight augmentation
```

Here, we have made a logical separation between the code that deals with event-related functionality in MainCore module and the rest of the code related to this module.

Notice that we have passed a reference of MainCore module (known to the application as `ImagesInc_Core`) to the IIFE that implements this augmentation (using tight augmentation technique) and then we have added new properties to MainCore module as needed. At the end, the reference to the now augmented MainCore module is returned to `ImagesInc_Core`, which is the global variable that provides access to MainCore module.

We use the same technique again in another part of the code to augment the module with more functionality. Please have a look at the related code in `MainCore.js` file of the application.

Augmenting MainCore using sub-modules

Let's look at an example of how we add sub-modules to MainCore module. To add enhanced logging functionality to the application, we have augmented MainCore module with a sub-module which specializes in logging messages for the application.

The following code snippet shows how this sub-module is being used by MainCore module:

```
mainCore.log = function(severity,msg, color){

        // if the logging module has been loaded, then use its full
    functionality
        // otherwise just log a simple message
        if(mainCore.LoggingHandler && mainCore.LoggingHandler.
    logMessage){

            mainCore.LoggingHandler.logMessage(severity,msg,color);

        }else{
            if(severity === 3){
                color = "color:red;font-weight:bold";
            }
            console['log']("%c Severity: " + severity + " ---> " + msg
    + " (From Core!)", color);
            }
    };
```

In this method, we first check to see if `LoggingHandler` object (the logging sub-module) exists and also if `logMessage` method on that object is implemented. If both conditions are met, then we pass on the logging message and its related information to this sub-module.

On the other hand, if the logging sub-module or its required method do not exit, we use `mainCore` module's own simple logging mechanism to log messages in the browser's console.

We should have a look at how `LoggingHandler` sub-module has been implemented and added to MainCore module.

Consider the following code snippet:

```
// using simple sub-module augmentation
ImagesInc_Core.LoggingHandler = (function(){

    var self = {}, messageParam, colorParam;
    self.logMessage = function(severity, message,color) {

    ....  ...

    return {
            logMessage: self.logMessage,
```

```
            initialize: self.initialize
    };
})();
```

As shown, we have added a property to `ImagesInc_Core` object (MainCore module). An IIFE returns an object to this property (`LoggingHandler`) when it is executed. This object consists of two methods which provide all the functionality related to the logging mechanism of the application.

While the implementation of these two methods is hidden away from the rest of the application, other pieces of the application can interact with this sub-module through MainCore module and the related interface.

Notice that this sub-module can easily be swapped for a different one or modified internally in any form that we desire. However, as long as the exposed interface does not change, all the external code would still be able to use this sub-module for its logging functionality.

In fact, we can even remove this sub-module completely and it will not affect the application at all, except for the fact that the advanced logging mechanism for the application would be absent. This highlights some of the advantages of modular design in our application, such as **plug-and-play**, **progressive enhancement**, and **graceful degradation**.

In the same way, we can also add other sub-modules to MainCore module to provide more functionality without the need to make many changes in the application. This allows us to have a flexible and easily maintainable code base.

In our application, there are also other sub-modules, which attach themselves to MainCore module, and provide added functionality to the application. We talked about these sub-modules in the previous chapter but I will mention them again here:

- `AjaxEngine`: This module is responsible for making AJAX calls to the server, using jQuery AJAX functionality.

- `CookieHandler`: This module looks after all the cookie-related operations in the application, such as writing, reading, and deleting cookies in the browser.

- `NotificationHandler`: This module is responsible for displaying notifications to the users by leveraging a dialog box component.

- `StorageHanlder`: All the functionality related to the browser's local storage that is implemented in this sub-module, such as storing, reading, and deleting objects in local storage.

- `Utilities`: This module provides helper methods to the application, such as methods to combine two objects, to see if an object is an array, to load files from the server, and so on.

Component registration with MainCore

Every component of our application is registered with MainCore module. This allows to create the bridge between the component and the application, by using an instance of SandBox module.. We will talk about the SandBox module shortly but let's have a look at how the registration of the components takes place in the application (in the MainCore module).

The following diagram provides an overview of this process:

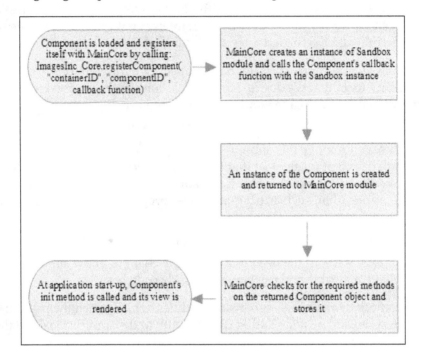

Consider the following implementation in MainCore module:

```
mainCore.registerComponent = function(containerID,
    componentID, createFunc){

        var containerElem, componentObj;

        // setting context for the sandbox
        if($){
            containerElem =  $("#" + containerID)[0];
        }else{
            containerElem = document.getElementById(containerID);
        }
```

```
        if(createFunc && typeof createFunc === 'function'){
            componentObj = createFunc(new
              SandBox(this,containerElem, componentID));
            //checking for required methods in component
            if (componentObj.init && typeof componentObj.init ===
              'function' && componentObj.destroy && typeof
              componentObj.destroy === 'function') {
                componentObj.id = componentID;
                registeredComponents.push(componentObj);

            }else{
                this.log(3,"Component does not have necessary
                  methods, thus not registered");
            }
        }else{
            this.log(3,"no creator function on
              component, component not registered");
        }
    };
```

As you can see, when this method is called at a component's load time by
the component, three parameters are passed into MainCore's `mainCore.`
`registerComponent` method: `containerID`, `componentID`, and `createFunc`.

`containerID` parameter is passed to this method to tell the application what
container (HTML element) the component's view needs to be rendered in.
`componentID` is the ID of the component that gets registered with the application
and `createFunc` is the callback function on the component, which `mainCore.`
`registerComponent` method calls to create an instance of the component.

We will talk about how components are instantiated in more depth, later in this
chapter. But for now, let's have a look at this mechanism from MainCore module's
perspective.

In the above method, we first walk the DOM tree to find the container element for
the component's view, either by using jQuery or the DOM API directly.

Then, we check to see if the required `createFunc` parameter has been passed in, and
whether it is a function. If so, we call this component's function with an instance of
`SandBox` module (using dependency injection). Remember that every component
gets a different instance of `SandBox` module, which is the bridge between the
component and the application.

This is done as follows:

```
componentObj = createFunc(new SandBox(this,containerElem,
componentID));
```

If the component is designed properly, the result of this function call is an instance of the component which is returned and stored in `componentObj` variable.

There are also a couple of required methods that we need to make sure exist on the component's instance: `init` and `destroy` methods. Notice that MainCore is not concerned with how such methods are implemented in the component or what they do, only that they exist. The internal implementation of such methods and what they do are the responsibility of the component itself and each component may implement these methods differently. Consider the following code snippet:

```
//checking for required methods in component
if (componentObj.init && typeof componentObj.init ===
   'function' && componentObj.destroy && typeof
   componentObj.destroy === 'function') {

        componentObj.id = componentID;
        registeredComponents.push(componentObj);

}else{
        this.log(3,"Component does not have necessary methods,
            thus not registered");
}
```

At the end of the registration phase, each component is pushed to `registeredComponents` array, which is a collection of all the registered components.

We use this array of components to do a few different things in the application. For instance, when the application is starting up, we loop through all the components in this array and call `init` method on each one of them. This is done as follows:

```
mainCore.initializeAllComponents = function(){

        this.log(1,"Initializing all components...", "orange");

        try{
            for(var i=0; i < registeredComponents.length; i++){
                registeredComponents[i].init();
            }

        }catch(e){
            this.log(3, 'APPLICATION CATASTROPHIC ERROR!' +
                e.name + ": " + e.message);
        }
```

```
        this.log(1,"All components have been
            initialized...", "orange");
    };
```

The preceding method of MainCore module is called in `index.html` file, as shown here:

```
    ImagesInc_Core.initializeAllComponents();
```

After `init` methods of all the components have been called by the application in the start-up phase, we will see the following messages displayed in the console, if the application is in debug mode.

```
Core Module has been initialized...
LoggingHandler Module has been initialized...
Utilities Module has been initialized...
CookieHandler Module has been initialized...
LocalStorage is availble.
StorageHandler Module has been initialized...
AjaxEngine Module has been initialized...
NotificationHandler Module has been initialized...
Initializing all components...
Core is listening to custom events now...
Header component has been initialized...
Footer component has been initialized...
Content component has been initialized...
NotificationHandler is listening to custom events now...
All components have been initialized...
```

Dynamic loading of components by MainCore

As you may recall, I mentioned previously that application components can be loaded at a later time than the application's start-up. MainCore module provides the hooks and implements the functionality needed to achieve this.

I think it might be a good idea to go back to the previous chapter and have a look at the flow diagram which depicts this mechanism before continuing with the explanations to follow, just so you can refresh your memory.

In our application, when the user clicks on the **Support** link provided in the footer section, a dialogue box is displayed. This dialogue box provides information regarding where the images of our application have been taken from and whether the user would like to visit that site.

This widget component (`notificationWidget`), is not loaded in `index.html` page when the application is initially started up; it is only loaded when the user clicks on the **Support** link.

However, if the widget has been previously loaded in the application (if the user had clicked on the **Support** link before), we will simply re-render it on the page. This is because after the first time this component is loaded, it will be kept in cache, even after the user closes the dialogue box by clicking on its **Close** button.

`NotificationHandler` sub-module is responsible for listening and acting on the click event of the **Support** link. This is done by using a publish-subscribe mechanism (pattern), which we will discuss shortly in this chapter.

Consider the following code snippet:

```
self.handleSupportClick = function(){
        // name of the component when it registers
          itselft with core is used here
        NotificationWidgetObj = ImagesInc_
          Core.getComponentByID("notificationWidget");
        if(!NotificationWidgetObj){
            ImagesInc_Core.loadComponent(ImagesInc_GlobalData
              .getNoficationWidgetDefID(), self.renderWidget);

        }else{
            self.renderWidget();
        }
    };
```

This method is the callback function for the **Support** link click event in `NotificationHandler` sub-module. The very first thing that this method does is to ask the application (MainCore module specifically) whether this component (widget) has been previously loaded and registered with the application, as follows:

```
NotificationWidgetObj = ImagesInc_Core
    .getComponentByID("notificationWidget");
```

If so, this methods calls `NotificationHandler.renderWidget` (`self.renderWidget`) function, which in turn calls `renderWidget` method on the widget component itself. Note that the widget is responsible for its own rendering, as shown here:

```
self.renderWidget = function(){
        ImagesInc_Core.getComponentByID("notificationWidget").
renderWidget();
    };
```

If the widget has not been loaded previously, the method asks the MainCore module to load the widget first, and then call `NotificationHandler.renderWidget` function, which is the callback function that is passed in as `self.renderWidget`.

This call is shown as follows:

```
ImagesInc_Core.loadComponent(ImagesInc_GlobalData
    .getNoficationWidgetDefID(), self.renderWidget);
```

Now the control is given to MainCore module to load the component (widget) dynamically. This is done by first finding the object definition for the component in the browser's local storage.

Let's first have a look at how the local storage is populated with the components' object definitions.

Storing object definitions in local storage

The application has been designed to find the object definitions for all the dynamically loaded components, in the browser's local storage.

However, these definitions are in fact implemented in `PageDefinitions.js` file.

When the `PageDefinitions.js` file is loaded, it uses an IIFE to store its object definitions in the browser's local storage, as follows:

```
(function(){

    var NotificationWidgetDefinition = {
        componentID: "notificationWidget",
        scriptFile: "NotificationWidget.js",
        scriptPath: "/js/Widgets/",
        cssFile: "NotificationWidget.css",
        cssPath: "css/"
    };

    ...

    ImagesInc_Core.saveValueToLocalStorage(ImagesInc_GlobalData
        .getNoficationWidgetDefID(),NotificationWidgetDefinition);

    ...

})();
```

After the browser's local storage is populated with the object definitions, the file is removed from the browser's cache as it can potentially be large and consume a significant amount of memory. This design allows us to minimize the use of the browser's cache, which could be of particular interest on mobile devices, where resources are limited.

Notice the object definition for `notificationWidget`. On this object, `ScriptFile` property holds the name of the `.js` file for this component and `ScriptPath` property stores the path to this file. MainCore module uses this information to find and load the component from the server.

Getting a component's object definition from local storage

Now that you know how the local storage is populated with the object definitions, we can look at how MainCore module gets the `notificationWidget` object definition from the local storage and loads the related resources.

Consider the following code snippet:

```
mainCore.loadComponent = function(ComponentDefID, callbackFunc){
        // get the value of Component object defintion from storage
        var ComponentDef =  mainCore.getValueForKeyAsObjectFromStorage
(ComponentDefID);
        loadedComponentcallbackFunc = callbackFunc;

        if(!ComponentDef){
            // if Component definition is not in the storage then the
page object definitions probably needs to be loaded
            mainCore.loadPageDefinitionsFileAndCallBack(
                function(){mainCore.getComponentObjAndCallback(
                ComponentDefID, mainCore.loadComponent
                FilesAndInitializeWithCallBack);});

        }else{
            mainCore.loadComponentFilesAndInitialize
                WithCallBack(ComponentDef);
        }
};
```

In this method, first the local storage in the browser is checked (using the `StorageHandler` sub-module behind the scenes) for the object definition of the component. If it is found, then this method calls another method to dynamically load the necessary resources for the component as follows:

```
mainCore.loadComponentFilesAndInitializeWithCallBack(ComponentDef)
```

Dynamically loading component's resources from the server

Once a component's object definition has been extracted from the local storage, its required .js and .css files are loaded from the server using the following method:

```
mainCore.loadComponentFilesAndInitializeWithCallBack =
    function(pageDefinitionObj, callbackFunc){
...

    mainCore.loadJSfileFromObjDefAndCallBack(pageDefinitionObj.
        scriptFile, pageDefinitionObj.scriptPath, function(){
        mainCore.initializeComponent(pageDefinitionObj
        .componentID, loadedComponentcallbackFunc)});


...

    mainCore.loadCSSfileFromObjDef(pageDefinitionObj.cssFile,
        pageDefinitionObj.cssPath);
...


}
```

As you can see, this method calls other methods which specialize in loading .js or .css files, as the mechanism for loading the files into the application is different, based on the file type. Of course the .js file is where the code for the component resides and the .css file has the styling-related information for the component.

Keep in mind that the callback function is called **asynchronously** after the files are loaded into the browser's cache.

Also, note that MainCore module uses Utilities sub-module (behind the scenes) to take care of the mechanics of requesting and loading the component files from the server.

The dynamic loading of components is probably the most involved operation in the application and it can be a little challenging to fully understand it by just reading this section. I highly recommend that you download the application's code and put breakpoints in the methods that I have mentioned in this section when you run the application. Doing so, will help you to fully realize how the flow of loading components dynamically is taking place.

After a component is dynamically loaded into the application, it still needs to register itself with MainCore module. We will talk about this process more later in this chapter.

Routing functionality in MainCore module

As our application is a single page application, and its view needs to change based on the user's interaction, we need to implement the client-side routing functionality. This also means that we need to incorporate page view changes based on the user clicking on the back and forward buttons of the browser.

In our application, I have used the HTML5 History API as the basis for our client-side routing, but we could have also used open source libraries such as `History.js` instead.

Let's see how routing functionality has been implemented in MainCore module.

Adding a URL to the history object of the browser

Consider the following method:

```
var addToHistory = function(dataObj){
    // if history object is supported
    if(!!(window.history && history.pushState)){
        history.pushState(dataObj,dataObj.url, dataObj.url);
    }else{
        alert('Your browser needs to be upgraded
            to the latest version');
        Core.log(3, "History API is not supported;
            from addToHistory");
    }
};
```

This method is called when the application needs to create an entry in the history object of the browser. For instance, when the **Home** link of the header section is clicked, the following callback function is called in the header component:

```
handleHomeClick: function (e) {
    sandBox.loadPage("index.html");
    e.preventDefault();
    e.stopPropagation();
    sandBox.addToHistory({
        url: "index.html"
    });
},
```

As you can see, the callback function calls `addToHistory` API of its `SandBox` instance with an anonymous object. The `SandBox` instance, in turn, calls `addToHistory` method of MainCore module. The anonymous object is passed to this method and then the browser's history object is updated, as follows:

```
var addToHistory = function(dataObj){

        // if history object is supported
        if(!!(window.history && history.pushState)){

            history.pushState(dataObj,dataObj.url, dataObj.url);

        }else{

            alert('Your browser needs to be upgraded
              to the latest version');
            Core.log(3, "History API is not supported;
              from addToHistory");
        }
};
```

There are three parameters which are passed to `pushState` API of the history object. These parameters are; `State` object, `Title`, and `URL`, respectively.

In our preceding example, the following object will be passed to this API as the first parameter:

```
{
        url: "index.html"
}
```

> Note that we use `url` property of the same object for the other parameters too.
>
> For more information regarding the browser's history API, you can refer to the following link:
>
> https://developer.mozilla.org/en-US/docs/Web/API/History_API

Getting a URL from the history object of the browser

To get URL entries from the browser's History object, we first bind `popstate` event of the browser to MainCore's `getFromHistory` method, as follows:

```
addEventHandlerToElem(window, 'popstate',getFromHistory);
```

This means that every time the browser's `pop` event takes place, which is when the user clicks on the back or forward button of the browser, the following method is called:

```
var getFromHistory = function(e){
      // if history object is supported
      if(!!(window.history && history.pushState)){
          if(e.state){
              Core.handlePageChange(e.state.url);
          }else if(e.originalEvent && e.originalEvent.state){
      // to get the original event in case of jQuery
              Core.handlePageChange(e.originalEvent.state.url);
          }else{
              Core.log(2, "Could not get the state of event
                from history object");
          }
      }else{
          alert('Your browser needs to be upgraded
            to the latest version');
          Core.log(3, "History API is not supported;
            from getFromHistory");
      }
};
```

The main action taken by this method is to call `handlePageChange` method of MainCore module. This method, in turn, publishes a `page-Changed` event in the application, as follows:

```
Core.handlePageChange = function(pageURL){
      Core.publishCustomEvent({
          type: 'page-Changed',
          data:pageURL
      });

};
```

When this event is published, all the modules that have registered for this event are notified. The modules can then take action based on the published event.

For instance, `content` component has bound `updateContentPage` method to this event as follows:

```
'page-Changed': this.updateContentPage
```

To better understand how this process works, we also need to talk about custom events and publish-subscribe (observer) pattern implementation in the application.

Publish-subscribe implementation in MainCore

As previously mentioned, one of the goals of our application design has been to create loose coupling among the application modules.

We have also talked about the fact that while our application modules are not aware of each other, they need to be able to communicate with one another in an indirect manner.

These goals can be achieved by leveraging the **Mediator** design pattern and implementing a publish-subscribe mechanism around that pattern.

As we saw in the previous chapter, in Mediator pattern pieces of the application do not directly register with each other for custom events. Instead, they register for these events and are notified of the broadcast of such events through an intermediary piece. In our application, the intermediary piece is our MainCore module.

> If you are not familiar with mediator or publish-subscribe patterns, I highly recommend reading, *Mastering JavaScript Design Patterns* by *Simon Timms*, which discusses many popular patterns as well as mediator pattern. You can find this book at the following link:
>
> https://www.packtpub.com/application-development/
> mastering-javascript-design-patterns

Registering components for custom events

The following method in MainCore module is used for registering components to receive custom events:

```
var registerForCustomEvents = function (componentID,eventsObj) {
    if (typeof componentID === 'string' &&
    typeof eventsObj === 'object') {
        for(var i=0; i< Core.registeredComponents.length ; i++){
            if(Core.registeredComponents[i].id === componentID){
                Core.registeredComponents[i].events = eventsObj;
                }
            }
        } else {
            Core.log(3,'Incorrect parameters passed in,
            from registerForCustomEvents');
        }
};
```

As you can see, this method registers the custom event object passed to it with the ID of the component, which needs to be notified when the event is published.

For instance, content component registers for the following events:

```
registerForCustomEvents : function(){
    sandBox.registerForCustomEvents({
        'img-Clicked': this.updateContentPage,
        // handles  image click
        'page-Changed': this.updateContentPage,
        // handles back and forward buttons
        'favorites-Clicked':this.updateContentPage
    });
},
```

When any one of the preceding events is published, the bound event handler method for that event is called.

Notice that in the code above, no component ID is passed to the SandBox module instance by the component. However, the SandBox module instance associated with this component sends the required component ID to MainCore module as follows:

```
registerForCustomEvents : function(eventsObj){
    if(eventsObj && typeof eventsObj === "object"){
        Core.registerForCustomEvents(componentID,eventsObj);
    }else{
        Core.log(3,"incorrect parameter passed in;
        from SandBox.registerForCustomEvents");
    }
},
```

We will talk about how the SandBox instance is aware of the component ID, when we talk about SandBox module later in this chapter.

Broadcasting custom events by components

When components need to publish custom events in the application, they do so by using publishCustomEvent method in MainCore module.

Consider the following code for this method:

```
var publishCustomEvent = function(eventObj){
    for(var i=0; i< Core.registeredComponents.length ; i++){
        if(Core.registeredComponents[i].events &&
        Core.registeredComponents[i].events[eventObj.type]){
            Core.registeredComponents[i].events[
            eventObj.type](eventObj.data);
        }
    }
};
```

As you can see, an event object is passed to this method. The method loops through all the components which have registered for this event and then calls the associated event handler on the components for the event.

Components can publish their events using their instance of `SandBox` module. For example, the `header` component of the application broadcasts that the Favorites link in the application has been clicked, as follows:

```
handleFavouritesClick: function (e) {

        e.preventDefault();
        e.stopPropagation();

    . . .

        sandBox.publishCustomEvent({
            type: 'favourites-Clicked',
            data: "favourites"
        });
        sandBox.addToHistory({
            url: 'favourites' //update url in the browser
        });
}
```

Since the `content` component has registered for this event, the method `updateContentPage` of the `content` component is subsequently called.

To sum things up, application components publish custom events, then the components that have registered for these custom events are notified by MainCore module, which calls the associated methods for these custom events. Thus, MainCore module acts as the mediator piece among all the components of the application.

This concludes our discussion and examination of the core module, but keep in mind that the core module as a whole provides many more capabilities for the application, beyond what we have discussed here. All such functionality is either implemented in MainCore module (`MainCore.js`) or other sub-modules which together, make up the core module.

Keep in mind that from the component's point of view, all the application functionality is provided by an instance of `SandBox` module.

SandBox module implementation

As mentioned previously, the components in our application do not directly communicate with each other nor do they communicate directly with any other parts of the application. The only connection between the components and the rest of the application is through an instance of SandBox module assigned to them.

SandBox module's constructor

Consider the following code snippet:

```
var SandBox = function(Core,contextElem, componentSelector){
    var Core = Core, containerElemContext =
    contextElem, componentID = componentSelector;

    return{
        getElement : function(elementID){
            if(elementID && typeof elementID === "string"){
                return Core.getElement(elementID);

            }else{
                Core.log(3,"incorrect parameters passed in;
                    from SandBox.getElement ");
            }
        },
    ...
    };
```

As the preceding code shows, SandBox module is created as a global object SandBox, and three parameters are passed to its constructor by MainCore module. Core parameter, which is a reference to MainCore module; contextElem parameter, which is a reference to the container element for the component's view that the SandBox instance belongs to; and componentSelector , which is the ID of the sandbox's component.

For instance, the SandBox instance of header component, receives the following parameters when it is instantiated: A reference to the core module as the first parameter, headerContainer which is the ID of header component's view container on the page as the second parameter, and header which is the ID of header component as the third parameter.

The reference to Core module is used by the SandBox module instance to get access to the functionality that Core module provides.

Setting a component's container context in the SandBox instance

A reference to the container element of the component's view is used by the `SandBox` module instance to set the DOM context of the component's HTML elements. This is so when an HTML element within this container needs to be accessed, the search for this element can start from the container element, as opposed to the `document` element of the page.

Have a look at the following code:

```
getElementInContext : function(elementID){
    if(elementID && typeof elementID === "string"){
        return Core.getChildOfParentByID(
        containerElemContext,elementID);
    }else{
        Core.log(3,"incorrect parameters passed in;
        from SandBox.getElementInContext");
    }

},
```

Here the `SandBox` module instance is calling the core module's `getChildOfParentByID` method. This method takes two parameters, `containerElemContext`, and `elementID`. The objective is to search the DOM tree for the element whose ID has been passed in.

Using the container element's DOM Context, we can start the search in the container of the component as opposed to the top-level element of the DOM tree. This approach allows us to have a much more optimized search for finding our component's elements.

Identifying the SandBox module's instance

The component ID, which is passed in as the third parameter to `SandBox` module's constructor, identifies the instance of `SandBox` module. This is used by the core module, to identify which component the `SandBox` instance belongs to.

For instance, the component's ID is used in the following method of SandBox module:

```
unregisterCustomEvent : function(eventType){

        if(eventType && typeof eventType === "string"){
            Core.unregisterCustomEvent(componentID,eventType);

        }else{

            Core.log(3,"incorrect parameter passed in;
                from SandBox.unregisterCustomEvent");
        }
    },
```

In the code snippet above, we are calling unregisterCustomEvent method of Core module and are passing in the parameter componentID. This is so core module knows which instance of SandBox is making this call and in turn, which component wishes to unsubscribe from the custom event.

SandBox module considerations

There are also a couple of other things that you need to keep mind about SandBox module. First, SandBox module can be designed to only provide a subset of Core module's functionality to the components. This enables us to control what application functionality components can have access to. Second, all the methods of SandBox module are designed to do a very basic error checking. This filter calls which that have passed the basic level of validation to propagate to Core module.

Keep in mind that SandBox module is supposed to be only a thin layer which sits between the components and the rest of the application. Thus, it is best to not do extensive validation at SandBox module level.

What constitutes a thin layer is open to interpretations, but since there could potentially be many instances of SandBox module in the application, it is best to keep it as thin as possible.

Application components

Considering that our application is a **proof of concept** type application, we have only implemented four components; header, footer, content, and notificationWidget (I'm using the component IDs used in the application).

These components are implemented in the following files in the application's project, `ImagesInc_Header.js`, `ImagesInc_Footer.js`, `ImagesInc_Content.js`, and `NotificationWidget.js`, respectively.

In the following sections, I will provide an overview of each component, but I highly recommend that you have a look at the code accompanying this book to get a better understanding of how these components are implemented.

Keep in mind that our components are modules, which create different application views. In an MVC or MV* architectural pattern paradigm, our components contain their own controllers as well as leveraging the application level controller which has been provided to them through their own instance of `SandBox` module.

The components also implement their own views and each component is only aware of its view in the application.

While an application level model is present (`ImagesInc_GlobalData`), and our components can use the data stored in this application model, each component can also contain its own model. Therefore, each component implements its own MVC or MV* architecture.

Registering components with MainCore module

We have already talked about how a component is registered with MainCore module from the MainCore's perspective. It is time to have a look at how this is done at the component's level.

The mechanism for registering components with the application is always the same, regardless of whether the component is loaded at the application start-up phase or at a later time.

Consider the following code snippet:

```
ImagesInc_Core.registerComponent("mainPageContainer",
"notificationWidget", function(sandBox){

    ...

    var widgetMainContainer, stockSnapURL =
    "https://stocksnap.io";

    return {
        init: function(){
            try{
                sandBox.contextObj = this;
```

```
            sandBox.logMessage(1,'Notification Widget
            component has been initialized...', 'blue');

        }catch(e){
            sandBox.logMessage(3,'Notification Widget has NOT
            been initialized correctly --> ' + e.message);
        }
    },

    destroy: function(removeComponent){

        sandBox.contextObj.unregisterFromEvents();
        if(removeComponent){
            sandBox.removeComponentFromDom("widgetContainer");
        }
        sandBox.logMessage(1,'Notification Widget has been
        destroyed...', "blue");
    },
    ...

}
```

As you can see, when a component's `.js` file is loaded, for instance `notificationWidget` shown previously, `registerComponent` method of MainCore module is called. Thus, MainCore module needs to be loaded before any component files in the application.

Since we have talked about how this method is called by a component previously, the following should be just a review for you.

In the preceding code, when `NotificationWidget.js` file is loaded, the `registerComponent` method of MainCore module is called with three parameters: `mainPageContainer`, which is the ID of the container element that hosts the component's view; `notificationWidget`, which is the ID of the component itself, and a third parameter as a `callback` function. When this `callback` function is called by MainCore module, it receives an instance of `SandBox` module.

Note that the return object from this callback function is the component's singleton object, which has the required methods `init` and `destroy`. Of course, these methods are used by the application to initialize and destroy the component instance, respectively. We will talk about these methods more when we talk about `notificationWidget` component.

One other thing to notice here is that we have created a closure in this callback function, so only the returned object from this function has access to the private variables of the component.

Header component

This component registers itself with Core module using the ID header, and from that point forward, this ID is used by the application to reference this component.

As with all the other components in the application, this component implements the required init and destroy methods.

header component also implements methods to attach and remove event handlers, for its elements. The method handleFavouritesClick is an example of an event handler in this component.

Consider the implementation of this event handler as follows:

```
handleFavouritesClick: function (e) {
        e.preventDefault();
        e.stopPropagation();
        var favoritedImagesArray = sandBox
        .getValueAsArrayFromCookie(ImagesInc_GlobalData
        .getFavCookieName());

        if(!favoritedImagesArray){
            alert('No favorites have been selected!');
            return;
        }
        sandBox.publishCustomEvent({
            type: 'favorites-Clicked',
            data: "favorites"
        });
        sandBox.addToHistory({
            url: 'favorites' //update url in the browser
        });
}
```

This method is called when the **Favorites** link of header component is clicked. It first checks to see if there are any favorite images stored in the browser's cookie. However, this check is not done directly by the component itself, as the call is made to the instance of SandBox module for this component.

Notice that header component has no idea how the mechanism for checking the cookie is implemented, and it does not need to implement such functionality itself.

If such mechanism is changed at some point in the future, it makes no difference to this component. The component will always make the same call to the `SandBox` module instance and lets the application handle this operation.

Also note that this method updates the URL in the browser, and publishes a custom event that informs the application of the particular event that has taken place. Of course, the component leverages the application's functionality through the `SandBox` module instance to accomplish all these tasks.

Footer component

The design of `footer` component is very similar to `header` component, and it registers itself with Core module with the ID of `footer`.

One method in the component which we need to have a look at is `hanldeSupportClick`. This method is called when the **Support** link of `footer` component is clicked. Let's examine the implementation of this method, as follows:

```
handleSupportClick : function(e) {

        sandBox.publishCustomEvent({
            type: 'support-Clicked',
            data: "support"

    });

    e.preventDefault();
    e.stopPropagation();
}
```

As you can see, when the link is clicked, the custom event `support-Clicked` is published. If you recall from an earlier section in this chapter, `NotificationHandler` module is listening to this event and will take the required action when this event takes place.

This is another example which shows, while these pieces of the application are communicating with each other, they are not actually aware of each other's existence. These components are loosely coupled using our publish-subscribe implementation.

Content component

This component can be considered as the main component of our application and it is responsible for changing the views of the content area. It registers itself with Core module with the ID of content.

The content component implements the required init and destroy methods as well as many other methods.

We are going to have a look at some of the important ones here.

Handling content area click events

When a user clicks on the **Add to Favorites** link in the application or when an image is clicked in the content area, the parent container of the content component's view captures the event and processes it.

The binding for the event handling of the parent container takes place in init method of content component as follows:

```
sandBox.addEventHandlerToParent("click",
    this.handleMainContainerClicked);
```

As you can see, handleMainContainerClicked is the callback method that processes this click event.

Consider how this method has been implemented:

```
handleMainContainerClicked: function (e) {
    if (e.target != e.currentTarget) {
        e.preventDefault();
        e.stopPropagation();

            if (e.target.tagName.toUpperCase() === 'IMG') {
                sandBox.contextObj.handleImageClick(e.target);
            } else if (e.target.tagName.toUpperCase() === 'A') {
                sandBox.contextObj.handelFavLinkClick(e.target);
            }
        }
    }
}
```

As shown, we check to see if the click event is taking place on an image or on an anchor tag, and based on this determination, we delegate the rest of the event processing to the associated methods.

Handling the Add To Favorite link click event

In `handelFavLinkClick` method, we check the state of the **Add to Favorites** link and change its text to **Remove from Favorites**. If the link has already been clicked, and it contains the text **Remove from Favorites**, we re-set the text to its default value of **Add to Favorites**.

We also add or remove the ID of the favorite image in the browser's cookie, so when the user navigates to the **Favorites** page, the correct favorite images are rendered in the content area.

Consider the implementation of this method:

```
handelFavLinkClick: function (elem) {
    var anchorState, parentNode, anchorID;
    anchorState = elem.getAttribute('data-state');
    anchorID = elem.getAttribute('id');
    parentNode = sandBox.getParentNode(elem);

    if (anchorState) {
        sandBox.removeValueFromCookie(favCookieName,anchorID);
        sandBox.updateElement(parentNode,
        sandBox.contextObj.getAnchorHTMLStr(anchorID));

    } else {
        sandBox.populateCookie(favCookieName,anchorID);
        sandBox.updateElement(parentNode,
        sandBox.contextObj.getAnchorHTMLStr(anchorID, true));
    }
    sandBox.publishCustomEvent({
        type: 'FavLink-Clicked',
        data: anchorID
    });
},
```

As you can see, there is also one other thing that we do in this method, which is to broadcast the related custom event to the application. This allows all the other pieces of the application which are registered for this event to be informed of the event taking place in this component.

Handling an image click event

When an image is clicked in the content area of the application, the following method is called:

```
handleImageClick: function (elem) {
        var imgName;

        imgName = elem.getAttribute('data-name');
        sandBox.publishCustomEvent({
            type: 'img-Clicked',
            data: imgName
        });
        sandBox.addToHistory({
            url: imgName
        });
    }
```

Notice that this method does two main things. One is to update the history object of the browser so that the application router can work properly when the user clicks on the back and forward buttons of the browser. The second is to broadcast the message img-Clicked to the application.

The interesting point to consider is that our content component itself listens to this event and acts on this event to update the page view, using the following event registration method:

```
registerForCustomEvents : function(){

    sandBox.registerForCustomEvents({
            'img-Clicked': this.updateContentPage,
        'page-Changed': this.updateContentPage,
            'favourites-Clicked':this.updateContentPage
        });
    }
```

As you can see, when img-Clicked event is received by content component (which itself had generated), then updateContentPage method of this component is called.

Of course, we could have directly updated the view of the page in handleImageClick method, but by broadcasting the event at the application level, we can be sure that all the pieces of the application, including content component itself, can take action upon the broadcast of this event.

Content area generator methods

content component also has methods which are responsible for generating the content area of the page, based on the URL of the browser. The following is a summary of such methods:

- buildFavouritesPage: This method loads the related CSS file for the Favorites page (using the SandBox module instance) and then renders this page based on the number of the favorite images previously selected by the user

- buildIndexContentHTML: As the name implies, this method is responsible for building HTML tags for the content area of index.html page

- buildImagePageHTML: The full view of the clicked image is rendered using this method

- getAnchorHTMLStr: This method generates the related link for each image so the image can be added or removed from the favorite images list, based on the state of the link

I highly recommend that you have a look at the code for this component to see how these methods are implemented.

NotificationWidget component

When this component is loaded, it registers itself as notificationWidget with core module.

We talked about this component previously and while its design is similar to all the other components in the application, there are some differences.

As mentioned before, this component is not loaded or rendered at the application's start-up phase. It is loaded and rendered dynamically only when needed, based on the user's interaction with the application.

NotificationWidget's model

This component's view is stored as a string in the component itself, as follows:

```
var widgetInnerHTMLStr = '<div id="notificationMainContainer">' +
    '<h1 class="centerElem header">Thank you for
        visiting us.</h1>' +
    '<h3 class="centerElem header">All the images
        on this site are provided by <a href="https://stocksnap.
io">stocksnap.io</a>.</h3>' +
    '<h3 class="centerElem header">We thank them and
        encourage you to visit their site.</h3>' +
    '<div class="buttonContainer">' +
```

```
    '<div class="button button-left" id=
      "notification_visit">Visit stocksnap.io</div>' +
    '<div class="button button-right"
    id="notification_close">Close</div>' +
  '</div>' +
'</div>';
```

This string is passed by the component to MainCore module to render its view. You will see how this is done very shortly.

Required methods of the notificationWidget component

As mentioned previously, each component needs to implement the required methods: `init` and `destroy`.

Have a look at the following `init` method of `notificationWidget` component as follows:

```
init: function(){
        try{
            sandBox.contextObj = this;
            sandBox.logMessage(1,'Notification Widget component
has been initialized...', 'blue');

        }catch(e){
            sandBox.logMessage(3,'Notification Widget has NOT been
initialized correctly --> ' + e.message);
        }
}
```

When the application calls `init` method of a component, in this case `notificationWidget`, a new property is added to the instance of `SandBox` module that was passed to the component. This property is `contextObj` and its value is set to `this`.

In this context, `this` is a reference to the component itself and is assigned to the `SandBox` instance so we can have an easy way to access the context of the component when we need to. This property is particularly useful for our event handler callbacks in the component.

Consider the following code snippet from `notificationWidget` component:

```
handleCloseClick : function(){
        sandBox.contextObj.unregisterFromEvents();
        sandBox.removeComponentFromDom("widgetContainer");
}
```

This callback function is called when the user clicks on the **Close** button of the dialogue box which is the view for `notificationWidget` component. You might wonder why we are not calling the component's internal method from the callback function as:

```
this.unregisterFromEvents();
```

For the above function call to succeed, the callback function needs to run in the context of the component. However, since the context of `this` is set at the time of code execution to the object that calls this callback function, and not the component, we are not be able to call the component's internal methods using `this`.

Thus, by setting the property `contextObj` on the `SandBox` instance, we are able to easily access the original context of the component and call the required internal method as:

```
sandBox.contextObj.unregisterFromEvents();
```

Of course, we could also use JavaScript's `bind()` method to achieve the same context preservation but I have used this approach instead, so you can see a different way of resolving this issue.

The `destroy` method of the component is used to make it inactive (no events on the component will be processed) or to completely remove the component from the DOM.

Consider destroy method implementation of `notificationWidget`, as follows:

```
destroy: function(removeComponent){

        sandBox.contextObj.unregisterFromEvents();

        if(removeComponent){
            sandBox.removeComponentFromDom("widgetContainer");
        }

    sandBox.logMessage(1,'Notification Widget has
        been destroyed...', "blue");

},
```

Depending on the value of `removeComponent` flag(`true` or `false`), which is passed to this method, the component is either disabled or completely removed from the DOM.

Note that in the above code, the component uses its instance of `SandBox` module to remove itself from the DOM and it does not need to implement such functionality itself. This allows the component to only focus on its own specialized tasks and leverage the functionality provided by the application (through the `SandBox` instance). This design also limits the component's access to the world beyond its own so we can minimize possible DOM manipulation conflicts, as described in the previous chapter.

Rendering notificationWidget

This component is rendered when `NotificationHandler` calls the render method of the component, as follows:

```
ImagesInc_Core.getComponentByID("notificationWidget")
  .renderWidget();
```

Consider the implementation of this method, as shown here:

```
renderWidget : function(){

    var generatedWidget;

    generatedWidget = sandBox.createDocument
      LevelComponent(widgetInnerHTMLStr);

    generatedWidget.id = "widgetContainer";
     sandBox.setElementContext(generatedWidget.id);
     this.registerForEvents();
},
```

The component uses a method on its instance of `SandBox` module to create a document level component (itself), in the following line of code:

```
generatedWidget = sandBox.createDocumentLevel
    Component(widgetInnerHTMLStr);
```

In turn, from the `SandBox` module instance, the following method on Core module is called:

```
var createDocumentLevelComponent = function(compnentViewStr){
    var mainComponentContainer;

    mainComponentContainer =  document.createElement("DIV");
      mainComponentContainer.innerHTML = compnentViewStr;
      document.body.appendChild(mainComponentContainer);

    return mainComponentContainer;

};
```

And a reference to the rendered component's view is passed back from Core module to `renderWidget` method of the component object. The rendered component's view is then tagged with an ID and its context is set on the `SandBox` module instance, as follows:

```
generatedWidget.id = "widgetContainer";
sandBox.setElementContext(generatedWidget.id);
```

Note that it is only at this stage that the component registers for events. This is different than other components in the application, which register for events when they are initialized. The reason is because when `init` method of this component is called, the component's view has not yet been rendered on the page. Therefore, there are no HTML elements for this component's view to attach events to. It is only after the rendering of the component's view that we can attach the required event handlers to the elements.

This widget is an example of how we can render and activate components in the application at any time, after the start-up phase.

GlobalData module

As the name implies, this module is designed to store application level data and act as the model for our application. It also provides public methods so that other modules can get and set data in this module. This module is defined as `ImagesInc_GlobalData` global variable in the application..

The following shows a snippet of the kind of data that the module stores:

```
var favCookieName = "Images_Inc",
    pageDefintionsFile = "PageDefinitions.js",
    pageDefinitionsFilePath = "js/Modules/PageDefinitions/",
...
```

This module is augmented with a sub-module `ImagesInc_PageSections`, which stores HTML markup strings related to `header` and `footer` components.

It is worth looking at how this sub-module is added to `GlobalData` module.

```
var ImagesInc_GlobalData = ImagesInc_GlobalData || null;

var ImagesInc_PageSections = (function(mainModule, subModule){
 // assigning the subModule if it is passed in
and also augmenting sub-module
```

```
    var pageSections = mainModule.pageSections =
    mainModule.pageSections || subModule;



...



})(ImagesInc_GlobalData || {}, ImagesInc_PageSections || {} );
// using Asynchronous sub-module
```

As you can see, we are using asynchronous sub-module augmentation technique to add the sub-module to GlobalData module.

This technique allows us to load GlobalData and its related sub-module (ImagesInc_PageSections) in any order that we desire without affecting the module's augmentation. The augmentation is different in comparison to how we added sub-modules to MainCore module in the application, as they could only be added to MainCore module after it was loaded.

Notice that we create the sub-module if it does not exist in the application when we execute the IIFE, as shown:

```
(ImagesInc_GlobalData || {}, ImagesInc_PageSections || {} );
```

Asynchronous sub-module augmentation also allows us to augment the sub-module itself, if it already exists in the application. The augmentation is shown in the following code snippet:

```
var pageSections = mainModule.pageSections =
mainModule.pageSections || subModule;

    pageSections.headerContainerDefObj = {

    sectionHTML :   '<div id="logoDiv" class="logo_titleClass" >' +
...


}
```

Admittedly, this technique is a little more complex than the other augmentation techniques that we have used elsewhere in the application but it does provide a greater degree of flexibility.

I encourage you to have a look at the code related to this sub-module (GlobalData_ Sub.js) to get a better understanding of how the technique works.

Summary

In this chapter, we had a closer look at our application's implementation and saw how all the pieces fit and work together to create our modular ecosystem, at the code level.

We examined how Core module (our application's controller) was created by leveraging different augmentation techniques and adding sub-modules to MainCore module. This approach allowed us to extend our application's capabilities with ease and in a modular way.

By creating instances of SandBox module, we established communication bridges among the components and the rest of the application while preserving the loose coupling principle of our design.

One important aspect of our application, is the ability to load components dynamically and we discussed how such functionality has been implemented in our Core module.

Using the publish-subscribe and mediator patterns, we created an event handing mechanism which all the pieces of the application can use to communicate with each other. This mechanism was also used in our client side router to change the views of the application.

At the end of the chapter, we created a global module to store our application level data and act as the model piece of our MV* design.

In the next chapter, we will discuss testing of our application's modules and will see how unit testing can help us maintain the integrity of our application during its development and operational phases.

Modular Application Design and Testing

9

Now that we have completed the implementation of our application, it is time for us to talk about testing it. Of course, we test our application to make sure things works
as expected and that the future changes to our code-base do not break our application's functionality.

One thing to keep in mind here, is that we are writing our tests after we have completed our implementation. However, there are times when we write our tests before our application's code.

The idea is that we write our tests first and expect them to fail since there is no implementation of the code. Then, as we implement our application, our tests start passing and we can be sure that the implemented code behaves as expected.

You may choose this approach over implementation first and testing later for your projects, but I would like to emphasize the point that, regardless of the approach, you need to write some automated tests!

With that in mind, in this chapter we are going to have a look at how we can write some unit tests, and how our modular approach in our application design makes writing automated tests easier and more maintainable. For brevity, we will only write unit tests for two of our modules but the principles discussed can be used to test our other modules too.

In this chapter we will cover:

- How our modules can be tested individually
- Writing tests without the need for third-party frameworks
- Improving and streamlining our unit tests using third party tools
- Using Jasmine as a testing framework
- Using Mocha and its related assertion libraries as a testing framework

Advantages of writing automated tests

As developers, our primary concern is to write code that can produce the expected functionality and results. While principle holds true, the way we achieve our final implementation goal is also very important.

A properly designed application is not just about achieving the final goal of the application but it should also be about implementing an easily extensible and maintainable code-base.

Using a modular approach certainly helps us with achieving such objectives but as we make changes to our code-base, and as our application goes through its life cycle, we need to make sure all the pieces of the application still work properly.

When we make a change to one part of the application, we need to make sure that the change does not adversely affect the other parts of our code base. Of course, one way of assuring this, is to test everything manually and check every aspect of our application under all the circumstance that it was designed for.. But such an approach is not only time-consuming, it is also very tedious as we need to go through the same process for every single change in our application.

Also, especially in big projects, other developers could be working on various pieces of the application. How can we be sure that their changes would not have undesired effects on the parts of the application that we are responsible for?

Automated tests enable us to check the functionality that we expect from our code base, either in a targeted manner for a particular piece of code or for the entire application as a whole. We write the tests once, and then can run them many times at will, either when there is a change in the code-base or on a continuous basis as part of our regular and testing process.

The other advantage of automated tests is that, as we are implementing our code, we get into the habit of considering how we can test the particular functionality using automated tests. This mindset results in writing better, more targeted and modular code.

Different types of automated tests

There are many different types of automated tests, but we will consider and talk about only three categories of such tests as listed here:

- Unit testing
- Integration testing
- End to end testing

Unit testing

Unit tests are usually designed to test the functionality of individual pieces of our code in isolation. This usually means testing our functions and methods, one at a time, to make sure they do exactly what is expected of them.

We usually write such tests in a manner that can verify the functionality of our methods and individual pieces of our code in various scenarios.

There are two main styles of writing unit tests; **Test Driven Development** (TDD) and **Behavioral Driven Development** (BDD).

Let's have a simplified overview of what they are and how they are different.

TDD unit tests

TDD unit testing is mostly used to test the implementation of our code. This is done by testing the actual result that a method produces against what is expected.

The TDD process can be thought of as the following loop, if we write our tests before the code implementation:

1. Write a unit test
2. Run the test and expect it to fail
3. Write the code required to make the test pass
4. Run the test again to make sure the test passes
5. Re-factor the code if needed
6. Start from the first step again

As you can see, TDD is meant to be implemented from the beginning of the project and to continue through the project's life cycle.

BDD unit tests

This style of testing is focused on the expected behavior of our code and not necessarily the implementation of it.

When we use BDD style of writing unit tests, we write our assertions in a way that can be read like a natural sentence.

For instance a test should read as, "returns a value that is incremented by 1 from the previous value".

BDD can also follow the same process loop shown in the TDD section.

TDD versus BDD

Imagine that we have a function which is a counter, and when it is called for the first time, it will return the value 1 and every time after that, it will return the previous counter value plus 1.

In TDD style of writing unit tests, we test that our function is initialized with the default value (start value) of zero, since that is tied with the very first time that the function is called.

This detail (that the start value is 0) is an implementation aspect, and TDD style of writing tests checks for such implementation details. It also means that if we decide the default value (start value) in our counter function should change to 2, our test case also needs to change accordingly.

In BDD style of writing unit tests, we don't check to see what the returned value is when the function is called for the very first time. We only check to see that every time the function is called the counter has been incremented by 1. This means that if we change the start value of the function at some later time, it has no effect on the expected behavior of the function. Our function should always increment the previous value by 1, regardless of the starting value.

The difference between TDD and BDD is very subtle but important to keep in mind.

In this chapter we will focus on writing unit tests in BDD style.

Test coverage

It is ideal to write enough unit tests to achieve 100 percent test coverage of our code. However, in reality, it is not always possible to write unit tests for every aspect of the code.

Of course, the more tests we write, the better the code quality we can expect, but time lines also need to be kept in mind for every project. In reality, we do not always have sufficient time to achieve the full coverage of our code base with unit tests. However, we should keep in mind that in the long run, we save more time on finding and fixing bugs when we have more code coverage with our tests.

In the absence of sufficient time, my recommendation is to make sure that you at least write unit tests for the core pieces of your application and cover them 100 percent. Then, if time permits, turn your focus to other non-critical pieces of your application and write as many unit tests as you can for those pieces.

This way, you can make sure of the quality and integrity of the application core and isolate possible issues in non-core and non-critical modules.

Integration testing

This type of testing is mainly focused on making sure that different pieces of the application can work together properly.

When different methods and modules are involved to provide a certain functionality, we want to test and see if the desired functionality has been achieved by the sum of collaboration among such pieces.

An example could be that one function reads a string from a file and passes it to another function, which creates an array based on the comma delimiter in the string. Our integration test will make sure that the correct array was produced based on these two functions working together to read and process the string.

End to end testing

These tests usually checks the flow of the application's functionality from the start to finish to make sure that the application as a whole is working properly and as intended.

For instance, to test the correct behavior of the application based on the form submission on a page, we can submit the form values to the server using an AJAX call, get the results from the server, and then refresh the content area of the application based on the returned values. By examining the final result, we can be sure that our application behaves as expected.

End to end (also known as **E2E**) testing is usually done after our unit tests and integration tests have passed.

A simple start to writing our unit tests

Writing unit tests is not about using the latest and greatest unit testing tools and libraries. It is simply about testing little pieces of the code in isolation. The simple fact which we should always keep in mind is that the main goal of unit testing is to ensure the proper functionality and integrity of our code. Even if you are not familiar with any unit testing tools, you can still write you own unit tests, using the skills that you already have in JavaScript.

However, as you will see later in this chapter, using third-party tools and frameworks can greatly help us to write better and more sophisticated tests.

For the rest of the chapter, we will target two of our sub-modules (CookieHandler and StorageHandler) and will write some simple unit tests for them. We will also explore how our modular architecture can help us write targeted and independent unit tests for each module.

Writing unit tests without any unit testing frameworks

While I don't recommend writing your unit tests without any help from third-party libraries and frameworks, my focus here is to get you started writing unit tests, regardless of whether you use a testing framework or not. Once you get started, you will slowly get used to the process and soon it will become a part of your regular development routine.

Thus, as a starting point, we will write our unit tests using plain JavaScript.

Adding an AppTester module to our application

As our client architecture is based on a modular design, we will continue with that approach and create a module that is responsible for running our unit tests.

Have a look at how I have structured this module in our project.

The `AppTester` module resides in the `AppTester.js` file, and adds itself to our MainCore Module (`ImagesInc_Core`) as a sub-module, as follows:

```
// adding AppTester as a sub-module
ImagesInc_Core.AppTester = (function(){
    function runAllUnitTests(){
        var testModule;
        for(testModule in ImagesInc_Core.AppTester){

            if(typeof ImagesInc_Core.AppTester[testModule]
              === 'object'){
                // run tests
                ImagesInc_Core.AppTester[testModule].runAllTest();
            }
        }
    }
    function reportTestResults(totalNumOfTest,
    passedNum, failedNum){
        var failTestMsgColor;
        failTestMsgColor = failedNum ? 'red':'pink';

        ImagesInc_Core.log(1, 'Total number of tests run:
        ' + totalNumOfTest, 'orange');
        ImagesInc_Core.log(1, 'Number of Tests Passed:
        ' + passedNum, 'green');
        ImagesInc_Core.log(1, 'Number of Tests failed:
        ' + failedNum, failTestMsgColor);
    }
    return {
        runAllUnitTests: runAllUnitTests,
        reportTestResults: reportTestResults
    };
})();
```

This sub-module exposes two methods: `runAllUnitTests` which runs all the unit tests that have been added to it and `reportTestResults` which is our unit test reporter responsible for displaying the result of our unit tests when they are run.

Notice that we are using the logging mechanism of our core module for reporting our test results, which demonstrates the re-usability of our modules and sub-modules in different contexts.

Adding unit test suites to our test-runner

We are going to add our unit tests to our test-runner `AppTester`, using the tight augmentation technique that you are now quite familiar with.

Generally speaking, it is a good idea to have at least one test file per module which contains all the related unit tests for that module in our application. As such, we have two files in our project; `CookieHandlerTester.js` and `StorageHandlerTester.js`. As the names imply, one of them holds all the unit tests related to `CookieHandler` sub-module and the other contains all the related tests for `StorageHandler` sub-module.

Keep in mind that if you create a large number of unit tests (the more, the better), you can further break down your unit tests into smaller chunks and files, which focus the different functionality of each module.

In our application, since we have a limited number of unit tests, we have kept all of them in their related files, one file per module.

In the following sections, we will only discuss one of them as they are both structured in a very similar manner.

CookieHandler module unit tests

The unit test suite related to our `CookieHandler` sub-module is added to the `AppTester` module as an object property. This enables our test runner (`AppTester`) to easily loop through all of our unit tests and execute them.

Consider the following code snippet:

```
ImagesInc_Core.AppTester = (function(mainTestModule){

    if(!mainTestModule){
        ImagesInc_Core.log(3, 'main test module not found!');
        return false;
    }
    var CookieTester = mainTestModule.CookieHandlerTester = {};
    var unitTests = [], totalErrors = 0, totalPasses = 0;

    //create a new value in the cookie
    unitTests[unitTests.length] = CookieTester
    .createCookie = function(name, value, decodeFlag){
        if(!name){
            name = "testCreateCookie";
        }
        if(!value){
            value = "testing for cookie";
```

```
        }
        if(!decodeFlag){
            decodeFlag = false;
        }
    ...
    return mainTestModule;

})(ImagesInc_Core.AppTester); // using tight augmentation
```

Note how we have added an object as a property to `AppTester` module.
This object (test suite) has all the related tests as its properties.

```
var CookieTester = mainTestModule.CookieHandlerTester = {};
```

Every individual unit test is added to this object, as follows:

```
CookieTester.createCookie = function(name, value, decodeFlag){
    ...
}
```

The array `unitTests` is used to run all of our tests using a loop when `AppTester`
module calls the `cookieTester.runAllTests` method, as follows:

```
// run all unit tests
CookieTester.runAllTests = function (){
        ImagesInc_Core.log(1, '*** RUNNING CookieHandler
        MODULE UNIT TESTS ***', 'orange');

        // run all unit tests
        for(var i=0; i< unitTests.length; i++){
          unitTests[i]();
        }

        //** test for negative result
        // should not be able to find the value
          below in the cookie specified
        CookieTester.findValueInCookie("testCreateCookie",
        "some value!", true);
        unitTests.length++;
        // should not be able to add the value
        to the cookie as it will be a duplicate
        CookieTester.addValueToCookie("testCreateCookie",
        "testing for cookie",false);
        unitTests.length++;
        mainTestModule.reportTestResults(unitTests.length,
        totalPasses, totalErrors);
        CookieTester.cleanup();
};
```

To run individual unit tests, we can call them by using their name identifier, directly on the `CookieTester` object, like so:

```
CookieTester.findValueInCookie("testCreateCookie", "some value!",
true);
```

That is why each individual unit test is added to both the `CookieTester` object and the `unitTests` array when defined, as follows:

```
unitTests[unitTests.length] = CookieTester.createCookie =
function(name, value, decodeFlag)
```

I highly recommend that you have a look at the code related to the `AppTester` and `CookieHandlerTester` modules in the accompanying project for this chapter to see how they are implemented.

Running CookieHandler unit tests

In our project setup, since we are not using an automated build system, we can add the functionality to our `index.html` and our core module to run all the unit tests when `index.html` is loaded in the browser.

Of course, we do not want to do this in a production environment. Usually, a good development environment leverages task runners such as **Grunt** or **Gulp** to run the unit tests as well as all the other client application build tasks such as linting, minifying and so on.

 If you are not familiar with these task runners, please check the following resources online:

http://gruntjs.com/

http://gulpjs.com/

In our environment, to run the unit tests, we call the following method in our `index.html` file:

```
ImagesInc_Core.runAllUnitTests();
```

`runAllUnitTests` method in our MainCore module, will use `AppTester` module to run all of our unit tests.

Consider the following implementation in our MainCore module:

```
mainCore.runAllUnitTests = function(){
        if(typeof ImagesInc_Core.AppTester !== 'undefined'){

            try{
                ImagesInc_Core.AppTester.runAllUnitTests();
            }catch(e){
                mainCore.log(3, 'AppTester ERROR! ' +
                e.name + ": " + e.message);
            }
        }else{
            mainCore.log(3, 'AppTester not available! ');
        }
    };
```

Here, we first check to see if `AppTester` module is present, and if so, we call `runAllUnitTests` method on that module.

In `AppTester` module, the code loops through all the unit test suites (in our case, unit tests for the `CookieHandler` and `StorageHandler` modules) which are the properties of the `AppTester` object. This is shown as follows:

```
function runAllUnitTests(){
        var testModule;
        for(testModule in ImagesInc_Core.AppTester){
            if(typeof ImagesInc_Core.AppTester[testModule] ===
            'object'){
                // run tests
                ImagesInc_Core.AppTester[testModule].runAllTests();
            }
        }
    }
```

In turn, this method calls the `runAllTests` method on each unit test suite as you saw earlier:

```
CookieTester.runAllTests = function (){
    ...
}
```

Because of our modular architecture, as we can add individual unit test suites for each module to our `AppTester` module; we can also remove them. This is done so in a similar way as we added `CookieHandler` test suite to `AppTester` but by removing the property related to test suite instead.

When we run our unit tests by loading `index.html`, we will see the following output in the browser's console (I'm using Chrome Development Tools).

```
*** RUNNING CookieHandler MODULE UNIT TESTS ***
createCookie has passed
populateCookie has passed
findValueInCookie has passed
addValueToCookie has passed
getCookieValueAsString has passed
getCookieValueAsArray has passed
removeValueByValue has passed
deleteCookie has passed
findValueInCookie has passed
addValueToCookie has passed
Total number of tests run: 10
Number of Tests Passed: 10
Number of Tests Failed: 0
```

I recommend that you try writing some of your own unit tests and adding them to the application's test suites.

All the needed setup for this has already been implemented for you in the accompanying code for this chapter.

Cleaning up after running our unit tests

It is always a good idea to design our unit tests in a way that they clean up after themselves, so any modification made either to the application or the environment is reset to its original state.

If you look at the code for both of our unit test suites, there is a clean-up method in each one of them that does just that.

Consider the following method in `CookieHandlerTester.js`:

```
CookieTester.cleanup = function(){
        ImagesInc_Core.CookieHandler.deleteAllCookies();
        totalErrors = 0; totalPasses = 0;
};
```

As you can see, since our unit tests add a few cookies to the browser, and manipulates them, we want to make sure that all the created cookies are removed and the environment is reset to its original state.

`CookieHandler.deleteAllCookies` method takes care of removing all the cookies in the browser.

Writing unit tests using third party frameworks

While it is possible to write our unit tests using only JavaScript and no third-party frameworks, it is a lot of manual work, even when writing a few simple tests.

Our approach in the previous section for writing unit tests was a good exercise but I think we can do much better by leveraging third-party frameworks designed specifically for this task. Such frameworks enable us to write more sophisticated tests with much less effort.

In this section, I'll introduce you to two very popular third-party frameworks, which allow us to write good, clean, and professional-grade unit tests.

The goal here is to give you a good starting point and provide you with a general overview of each library, but we will not explore any of them in great depth. Nevertheless, I'm hoping to get you excited enough about using third-party unit testing libraries (frameworks) that you will spend some time getting to know them better on your own and use them in your future projects.

Introduction to Jasmine

Jasmine defines itself as "a behavior-driven development framework for testing JavaScript code."

Jasmine does not require a DOM and can be used for writing and running JavaScript unit tests both on the server and client side.

Setting up **Jasmine** is easy, especially on the client side, and is created in a way that provides all the functionality that you may require from a professional-grade testing framework in one package. I think you will find the syntax quite intuitive and easy to follow.

I personally like Jasmine quite a bit and am very grateful to its creators for providing us with such a great tool.

 In this section, I'll be using Jasmine 2.4 and encourage you to visit the related site at: `http://jasmine.github.io/`.

Setting up Jasmine

When you visit Jasmine's site, you will be presented with a link to download the standalone version of the framework, which is the version that we will be using for our unit tests here.

After downloading the zip file, and extracting its contents, you will see the following structure:

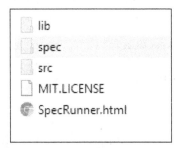

We will be using a similar file structure for our tests, however, without the need for the src folder, which is the location of the source files that Jasmine loads to run the tests against.

In our tests, we will be loading MainCore module and CookieHandler module directly from where they reside currently in our project.

The lib folder is where all the source code for Jasmine itself is kept and the spec folder is where we will store our test specs.

Here is how the final file structure has been implemented in our application:

In order to load our test specs in `SpecRunner.html`, we need to make the following modifications to this file, as follows:

```html
<script src="lib/jasmine-2.4.1/jasmine.js"></script>
<script src="lib/jasmine-2.4.1/jasmine-html.js"></script>
<script src="lib/jasmine-2.4.1/boot.js"></script>

<!-- include source files here... -->
<script type="text/javascript" src="../Core/MainCore.js" ></script>
<script type="text/javascript" src="../Core/CookieHandler.js" ></script>

<!-- include spec files here... -->
<script src="spec/cookieHandlerSpec.js"></script>
```

As you can see, we have pointed `SpecRunner.html` to the file locations of our `MainCore` and `CookieHandler` modules in the application, instead of using the default Jasmine `src` folder.

That is all we have to do to get Jasmine set up and ready for use in our client application.

Why load MainCore.js?

As you may have noticed in `SpecRunner.html`, I'm loading both the `MainCore.js` and `CookieHandler.js` files. This is not necessary, as long as `CookieHandler.js` returns a global object, which can then be used in `CookieHandlerSpec.js` to run the tests against. In such a scenario, `CookieHandler` object will act as an independent module, thanks to our modular architecture. However, to keep the code as is, I load MainCore module first and then use `CookieHandler` as a sub-module of MainCore; thus both files need to be loaded.

Creating our Jasmine spec file

To write and run our tests, we need to first create the structure of our spec file. We do this by implementing our test suites.

A test suite is constructed using `describe` function of Jasmine framework. This function takes two parameters, a string which describe the test suite and a callback function used to implement the test suite itself. This is shown below:

```
describe("Testing cookieHandler Sub-module", function() {
    . . .
}
```

Inside the callback function is where we write our test specs. Keep in mind that we can nest `describe` functions too. This means that we can use one `describe` function to create a test suite for the whole module and use nested `describe` functions inside that to create test suites for each individual method of the module. Also, any variables that we declare inside a `describe` function is available to all the specs which reside inside that `describe` block.

Let's have a look at our first spec for `CookieHandler` sub-module:

```
describe("Testing cookieHandler Sub-module", function() {

    var cookieHandler = ImagesInc_Core.CookieHandler;
    describe("createCookie Method", function() {
        it("should exist", function() {
            expect(cookieHandler.createCookie).toBeDefined();
        });
    ...
}
```

As you can see, we have used the outer `describe` function to encapsulate all the unit tests related to `CookieHandler` sub-module. Inside that, we are using another `describe` function to write the related specs for `createCookie` method of this sub-module. The `it` function is where we write our expectations, which are our assertions about the method that we are testing.

The expectations use matchers to implement a comparison between the actual value and the expected value. Jasmine comes with a slew of built-in matchers but it also provides us with the ability to write our own custom matchers.

In the code snippet above, we are telling Jasmine to check to see if `cookieHandler.createCookie` has been defined.

Notice how we are describing our tests using strings passed to `describe` and `it` methods. When the tests are run, these strings should read like sentences, describing what our tests are, and what kind of results we should be expecting from running such tests.

Important point to keep in mind when writing unit tests

Ideally, we want each unit test to only test one functionality, and not have any dependency on another functionality in the code. For instance, if we want to test that a method can read from a cookie, we should only test that and not if we can write to the cookie first, and then read the value, all in one test spec. In some of our specs we have not followed such a rule. To eliminate these types of dependencies, we need to use **spies**, **stubs**, and **mocks** which require more in-depth knowledge of our testing frameworks as they are considered more advanced features. Since, this is only an introduction to unit testing, such advanced functionality of the frameworks are beyond the scope of this book, but I highly recommend that you research them further on your own as such features are very useful in writing unit tests.

Running our Jasmine unit tests

We can run our unit tests by loading `SpecRunner.html` in the browser. When our tests have completed running, we will see the following results displayed in our browser window:

```
⊛ Jasmine  2.4.1
. . . . . . . . . . . . . . . . . . . .

20 specs, 0 failures

Testing cookieHandler Sub-module
  createCookie Method
    should exist
    should return false, when no cookie Name is passed
    should return false, when no cookie Value is passed
    should return undefined when cookie name and value have been passed
    should create a cookie
  getCookieValueAsString Method
    should exist
    should return false, when no cookie Name is passed
    should return null when the cookie is not found
    should return the value of the cookie correctly
  populateCookie Method
    should exist
    should return false, when no cookie Name is passed
    should return false, when no cookie Value is passed
    should return true when cookie name and value have been passed
    should call getCookieValueAsString
    should create a new cookie
    should add a new value to the existing cookie
    should NOT add a duplicate value to the existing cookie
  deleteAllCookies Method
    should exist
    should return true after removing all cookies
    should not have any cookies for the domain
```

As you can see, the sentence in our test suite tells us what method the group of tests belongs to, and the sentence in our assertion tells us what the test is for.

Our results show that all of our tests are passing. If one of our tests fails, Jasmine notifies us as follows:

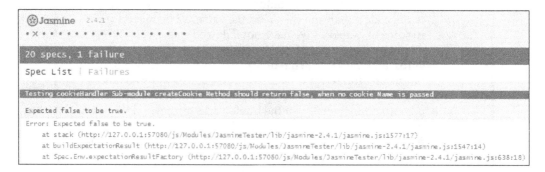

The message shows us what test has failed along with a stack trace related to that test. This allows us to quickly identify the failing test and look into what needs to be done to fix it.

Exploring Jasmine further

Jasmine is a complete testing framework for JavaScript. My goal was to only introduce you to it, and give a very quick overview of some of its capabilities. However, Jasmine provides much more functionality to satisfy any testing needs that you might have, such as using **spies**, **stubs**, and **mocks**, as well as support for asynchronous testing.

I recommend that you first have a look at the test suite that I have created for our `CookieHandler` sub-module, in the code accompanying this chapter. Then, go to Jasmine's website and learn more about the framework. I think once you start using Jasmine, you will be very impressed with its capabilities and ease of use.

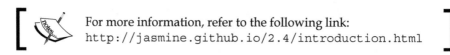

> For more information, refer to the following link:
> http://jasmine.github.io/2.4/introduction.html

Introduction to Mocha

Mocha is another great testing framework which allows us to use any assertion library that we like, and provides great flexibility in that aspect. As indicated on Mocha's website, *"if it throws an error, it will work!"*.

We will be using **Chai** assertion library in our tests and we will talk about this library very shortly.

Mocha can be run both on the server and the client side and it supports both BDD and TDD style tests. We can also use different reporters with Mocha, such as **Dot Matrix** and **List**.

For our purposes, we will be focusing on how to run Mocha in the browser.

Setting up Mocha

To set up Mocha for running our tests in the browser, we can use `sample.html` file that Mocha provides on its website.

In this file, Mocha is loaded using a **content delivery network** (**CDN**). We can also download the framework from GitHub, at: `https://github.com/mochajs/mocha`.

For our application, I have downloaded Mocha and created the following structure in the project:

In the preceding screenshot, `MochaRunner.html` is our test-runner page and loads Mocha, Chai (the assertion library), our source file (`StorageHandlerSpec.js`), and the related spec file, `storageHandlerSpec.js`. This file stores all of our Mocha tests.

This is how our `MochaRunner.html` is set up:

```
<script src="lib/mocha.js"></script>
<script src="lib/chai.js"></script>

<!-- include source files here... -->
<script type="text/javascript" src="../Core/MainCore.js" ></script>
<script type="text/javascript" src="../Core/StorageHandler.js" ></script>


<script>mocha.setup('bdd')</script>
<script src="./spec/storgeHandlerSpec.js"></script>

<script>mocha.run();</script>
```

As you can see, we are also telling Mocha that we will be using BDD style test specs.

This is all we have to do to implement a simple setup for Mocha.

Chai

Chai is a very popular assertion library that integrates well with Mocha and provides different assertion styles. In my opinion, one of the best assertion styles to use is **Expect**.

I think you will find Expect syntax similar to Jasmine assertion syntax and easy to understand.

 To use Chai, you can simply download the code (copy/paste) from the following location and add it to your project:

`http://chaijs.com/chai.js`

As you saw previously, I have already downloaded and installed Chai in the project library and it is ready for us to use.

Creating our Mocha spec file

The setup for a Mocha `spec` file is very similar to Jasmine's spec file. We create our test suites using the global `describe` function and pass it a callback function which contains the code for our assertions.

Just as with Jasmine, we use strings to identify our tests and use `it` function to write our assertions. Also, similar to Jasmine, we can use nested `describe` blocks, and any variable defined in a `describe` block is available to all the assertions in that block.

Have a look at the following code snippet from our `storageHandlerSpec.js` file as follows:

```
var expect = chai.expect;
describe("Testing storageHandler Sub-module", function() {
    var storageHandler = ImagesInc_Core.StorageHandler;

    describe("saveValueToLocalStorage Method", function() {
        it("should exit", function() {
          expect(storageHandler.saveValueToLocalStorage).to.exit;
        });
    ....
});
```

Note that we have set the variable `expect` on `chai.expect` global object, and then this variable is used in our assertions.

Chai provides a great set of matchers which we can use in writing our unit tests. However, the set of matchers provided by Chai is not as complete as Jasmine.

For instance, to use spies, stubs, and mocks, which are considered more advanced testing features, we need to use a different library such as **Sinon**.

Since such features are beyond the scope of this book, we will not explore them here but I encourage you to visit Sinon's web site for more information at: `http://sinonjs.org/`.

Running our Mocha-Chai unit tests

If we load our project's `MochaRunner.html` file in the browser, we will see the following test results displayed, after all the tests are run:

Index

Testing storageHandler Sub-module

saveValueToLocalStorage Method
- √ should exit
- √ should return false when no key is passed in
- √ should return false when no value is passed in
- √ should create value for the key in the local storage
- √ should return true when the value is created in the local storage

getValueForKeyAsString Method
- √ should exit
- √ should throw error when no key is passed in
- √ should return false when the key does not exist in local storage
- √ should return the correct value from local storage

checkLocalStorageForkey Method
- √ should exit
- √ should return false when the key does not exist in the local storage
- √ should return true when the key exists in local storage

replaceValueForKey Method
- √ should exit
- √ should return false when the key is not passed in
- √ should return false when the value is not passed in
- √ should replace value with the new value

removeKeyFromStorage Method
- √ should exit
- √ should remove key from local storage

clearLocalStorage
- √ should exit
- √ should remove ALL keys from local storage

Of course, the check marks beside our tests indicate that the tests have passed.

The following image shows the page when one of our tests fails:

```
saveValueToLocalStorage Method
    ✓ should exit
  ✗ should return false when no key is passed in


    AssertionError: expected false to be true
        at Context.<anonymous> (spec/storgeHandlerSpec.js:15:25)


  ✗ should return false when no key is passed in


    AssertionError: expected false to be true
        at Context.<anonymous> (spec/storgeHandlerSpec.js:15:25)
```

As you can see, to report a related error, Mocha uses the string that we have passed to it function of our test spec.

Exploring Mocha further

Using Mocha in conjunction with Chai and Sinon enables us to create a robust testing framework. We can even go beyond that by leveraging Mocha on the server side as part of our client's build system. This allows us to set up and run our tests automatically as one of the build steps, using **Node.js**. Furthermore, while not specific to Mocha, using **GitHub** as our source repository enables us to upload our Mocha tests into GitHub and have our tests run automatically in various browsers.

 You can get a lot more information regarding this feature at the following site:

https://ci.testling.com/

Summary

In this chapter, we talked about various types of tests and why continuous testing of our code is important to the integrity of our application as a whole. One of the ways to implement continuous testing is using unit tests.

We explored how we can write some simple unit tests using plain JavaScript and saw that using third-party testing frameworks enables us to have more capable and robust tests in our application, with much less effort.

Using a modular architecture, allows us to easily test our modules in isolation and to quickly find and fix possible issues in our code.

We also glanced over two very popular open source testing frameworks, Jasmine and Mocha. However, we barely scratched the surface of the capabilities that these frameworks offer, and I encourage you to explore them further on your own.

All the tests shown in this chapter are included in the source code accompanying this book, and I highly recommend that you have a look at the test suites and spend some time to become familiar with them.

In the next chapter, we will look at different approaches for loading modules into our application and see how we can manage module dependencies using industry's best practices.

10
Enterprise Grade Modular Design, AMD, CommonJS, and ES6 Modules

In this last chapter of the book, we are going to mainly focus on re-factoring some of our application modules so we can have a more robust way of loading and managing them.

The title of this chapter mentions Enterprise Grade, but in fact we can use the principles discussed here for applications of any size and type. In the next sections, I'll introduce you to various approaches for creating and loading modules in JavaScript and talk about the environments that each approach might be better suited for. You'll also see how we can manage our module dependencies in a more structured manner.

Keep in mind that this chapter is meant to be only an introduction to such techniques, but hopefully it will make you curious enough to research them further.

I believe after seeing their benefits, you'll consider these modular design implementations in your future projects.

Some of the topics that we will cover in this chapter are:

- Why we need a better setup for loading our modules
- AMD module format and how to use it
- Tools for creating AMD modules
- CommonJS module format
- ECMAScript 6 modules

Revisiting index.html file

If you recall, in *Chapter 8, Application Implementation – Putting It All Together*, I mentioned that we were using quite a few `<script>` tags in our `index.html` file to load our application's modules.

To refresh your memory, here is what we had:

```html
<!--loading base and GlobalData modules-->
<script type="text/javascript"  src="js/Modules/Base/Base.js" ></script>
<script type="text/javascript"  src="js/Modules/Base/jquery-1.10.2.min.js" ></script>
<script type="text/javascript"  src="js/Modules/GlobalData/GlobalData_Sub.js" ></script>
<script type="text/javascript"  src="js/Modules/GlobalData/GlobalData.js" ></script>

<!--loading app core modules-->
<script type="text/javascript"  src="js/Modules/Core/MainCore.js" ></script>
<script type="text/javascript"  src="js/Modules/Core/Logger.js" ></script>
<script type="text/javascript"  src="js/Modules/Core/Utilities.js" ></script>
<script type="text/javascript"  src="js/Modules/Core/CookieHandler.js" ></script>
<script type="text/javascript"  src="js/Modules/Core/StorageHandler.js" ></script>
<script type="text/javascript"  src="js/Modules/Core/AjaxEngine.js" ></script>
<script type="text/javascript"  src="js/Modules/Core/NotificationHandler.js" ></script>
<script type="text/javascript"  src="js/Modules/SandBox/SandBox.js" ></script>

<!--loading app components-->
<script type="text/javascript"  src="js/Components/ImagesInc_Header.js" ></script>
<script type="text/javascript"  src="js/Components/ImagesInc_Footer.js" ></script>
<script type="text/javascript"  src="js/Components/ImagesInc_Content.js" ></script>
```

While this implementation worked, it was not very scalable, since for each module file we needed to add a `<script>` tag to our page. Also, by looking at the list of files being loaded, we could not determine how each module or component was dependent on another piece (or pieces) of the application.

We had to create another `<script>` tag at the bottom of the page as well, which took care of booting-up the application, as shown here:

```html
<script type="text/javascript">

    ImagesInc_Core.initializeAllModules();
    ImagesInc_Core.initializeAllComponents();
    ImagesInc_Core.handlePageChange(location.pathname);

</script>
```

It would be nice if we could eliminate the need for having all the `<script>` tags and our boot-up sequence in `index.html`. Also, it would be very useful to implement a mechanism which could indicate and mange our modules' dependencies.

Well, we are going to achieve all that very soon!

The following screenshot depicts how the new approach will clean up our `index.html` file and provide us with a more robust script-loading capability:

```html
<:DOCTYPE html>
<html lang="en">

    <head>
        <meta charset="UTF-8">
        <meta name="viewport" content="width=device-width, initial-scale=1.0">
        <title>Images Inc.</title>
        <link rel="stylesheet" href="css/app.css">
    </head>

    <body>

        <header id="headerContainer" role="banner" itemscope itemtype="https://schema.org/WPHeader" class="headerContainerClass">
        </header>

        <main id="mainPageContainer" role="main" class="clearfix mainPageContainerClass">
        </main>

        <div id="footerParentContainer" class="footerContainerClass" >
            <div id="footerContainer" class="footerlinksContainerClass">
            </div>
        </div>

        <!--loading all the pieces of the application and booting it up -->
        <script src="js/lib/require.js" data-main="js/config"></script>

    </body>

</html>
```

As you can see, the page has been shortened considerably and there is only one JavaScript file that is loaded in `index.html` now. This file is `require.js`, with its data-main attribute set to `js/config`, as shown here:

```html
<script  src="js/libs/require.js" data-main="js/config"></script>
```

Loading this script is all we need to do in order to load all of our modules and components, and to start up the application.

We will have a look at how this magic has taken place shortly, but before doing so, we need to talk about **AMD** modules.

Introducing Asynchronous Module Definition

Asynchronous Module Definition (AMD) format for creating modules in JavaScript, is targeted for use in browsers. This format proposes a particular way for defining modules so that modules and their dependencies can be loaded into the browser asynchronously.

There are two key methods that you need to use when creating and consuming AMD modules, these are `define` and `require` methods.

The idea is that we create a module using the global `define` method and then we can import that module in other parts of the code (other modules) using the global `require` method.

Defining modules using AMD format

Here is how a module can be defined in AMD format:

```
define('moduleOneId', ['dependency'], function(dependency) {

    return {
        sayHi: function(){
            console.log('Hi there!')
        }
    }
});
```

In the preceding code, we are passing three arguments to the global `define` method, which has been provided to us by an AMD-compatible module loader.

The first argument, `moduleOneId`, is an optional parameter which assigns an ID to the module. Most of the time, we do not use this argument and other than some edge cases or when a non-AMD concatenation tool is being used to bundle our code, we leave it empty.

The second argument to `define` function is an array of dependencies, which tells the AMD module loader what modules (files) need to be loaded before executing the callback function. Of course, the third argument passed to `define` method is the callback function.

Notice that we are returning an object from this callback function. This object is the module that we are defining. In AMD format, the callback function can also return constructors and functions.

Importing AMD modules

To use the module that we have defined in the preceding code, we can import it by using the global `require` function.

Consider the following:

```
require(['moduleOneId'], function(moduleOne){
    moduleOne.sayHi();
});
```

Here, we are asking the AMD module loader to load the dependency `moduleOneId` before executing the callback function.

Note that we could also use the path to our dependency instead of using the related ID. For instance, we could write the preceding code snippet as follows:

```
require(['folderPath/moduleOne.js'], function(moduleOne){
    moduleOne.sayHi();
});
```

AMD format provides great flexibility in defining and loading our modules. It also eliminates the need for creating global variables to define the modules. AMD-compatible script loaders also often provide the capability to lazy-load our modules, if needed.

There are many web development tools (libraries) that support AMD format, but the most popular ones are `RequireJS` and `curl.js`.

In our application in this chapter, we will be using `RequireJS` to create our AMD modules and load their dependencies.

 For an in-depth discussion on JavaScript modules and their related formats, I encourage you to visit a great post by *Addy Osmani* at https://addyosmani.com/writing-modular-js/.

Introducing RequireJS

As mentioned previously, one of the most popular AMD module loaders for the browsers is **RequireJS**. In this section, we will learn how to create and load modules using this tool.

You can also run RequireJS on the server side using its related optimizer, `r.js`. The optimizer can package all of our AMD modules into one file and then the browser will only have to make one request to the server to load all the necessary modules. In this scenario, AMD format is used to manage dependencies among modules when they are being bundled on the server.

Alternatively, if you are using a server build setup for your client files, you may want to consider using `almond.js` for packaging your AMD modules. This is a much smaller library, but does not have the dynamic loading capabilities of RequireJS. For more information regarding `almond.js`, visit the following URL: `https://github.com/requirejs/almond/`.

Since we are not using a build system for our project, I will only cover using `RequireJS` for the browsers in this chapter.

Downloading RequireJS

We can download this library from the following location: `http://requirejs.org/docs/download.html#requirejs`.

You can simple copy the minimized version of the tool and save it in your selected file location.

A test project for creating and loading AMD modules

To help you become more familiar with RequireJS, I have included an additional project called **requireJsLearning** in the source code related to this chapter. I encourage you to download this project and follow along as we continue our talk regarding AMD
and RequireJS.

In `requireJsLearning` project, I have saved the RequireJS library (`require.js`) in the `libs` folder, as shown here:

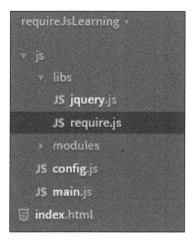

Let's create some simple modules in this project and see how we can use RequireJS to load and manage them.

Creating a simple AMD module

We start by creating a simple AMD module in `person.js` file, under `modules` folder.

Consider the following:

```
define(['modules/stuff', 'jquery'], function(stuff, jq) {
    console.log(jq + "  --> Accessing jQuery from person");
    return {
        first: "Sam",
        last: "SamLastName",
        favorites: stuff.likes.join(' ')
    }
});
```

In the preceding code, we are using the global `define` method that RequireJS has provided for us and passing two parameters to it. The first parameter is an array with two values. The first value in this array is a path to another module, which is a dependency for our `person` module.

Notice that we are using the name of the file but without the `.js` extension. This is because RequireJS assumes the extension to be `.js` by default.

The second value in our dependency array is **jQuery**. We are not specifying a path for jQuery here, as it is being used as a global variable.

> **jQuery and AMD format**
>
> As of version 1.7, jQuery supports AMD format. However, for it to be loaded properly as an AMD module, we can only place it in the same location as our `config.js` file. Since we would like to have all of our third-party libraries under `libs` folder in our project, we need to do a little bit of configuration. We will talk about this shortly.

The second parameter passed to `define` method is the callback function that gets executed after our `person` module's dependencies are loaded.

As the preceding code shows, this callback function receives two parameters, which are matched one-to-one to the dependency list defined for the `person` module.

We also return an object from this callback function which is our `person` module that can be consumed by other modules.

Consuming our person AMD module

Since `person` module is created as an AMD module, we can consume it as a dependency in other modules by only specifying its path.

Have a look at how our `main` module (in `main.js`) requires and uses `person` module, as shown in the following:

```
// bootstrap file
require(['modules/person', 'jquery', 'person2'],
function(person, $$, person2){

    console.log("Accessing Person --> person first + person last;
    from main -> " + person.first + ' ' + person.last);
    console.log($$ + "  --> jquery from main");
    console.log("Accessing person2 --> person2.first ;
    from main -> " + person2.first)
});
```

The preceding syntax should be a lot more familiar to you now. We are telling RequireJS (using `require` method) to load all the dependencies listed in the dependency array (the first argument to `require` method) and then pass them as arguments to the callback function.

RequireJS in turn, will make asynchronous calls to the server (one call per module) to download all of the dependencies.

Loading dependencies of dependencies

Notice that our main module has listed person module as a dependency. However, person module itself has also listed stuff module as a dependency:

```
define(['modules/stuff', 'jquery'], function(stuff, jq) {
...
}
```

Therefore, there is a dependency chain that needs to be resolved. When RequireJS looks for the dependency list of main module and sees person as a dependency, it then looks to see if person has any dependencies itself. If so, it will load those dependencies first. After that person module is loaded and passed to main module.

We can think of this chain as follows:

Load stuff module | pass it to person module | load person module | then pass person module to main module.

This is a very simplified view of how RequireJS manages dependencies and loads modules in the correct order, based on the dependency list.

A small but important point

In the preceding explanation, I mentioned the order of how modules get loaded based on the dependency list. The fact is that these modules can be physically loaded in a different order, but the important point to keep in mind is that all of the modules listed in the dependency list are loaded and the code in them is executed *before* the callback function is called.

Loading and consuming non-AMD modules

We also need a way to load non-AMD modules or non-modular files in our projects, and RequireJS provides hooks to do just that.

It also has many plugins which enable us to load CSS and text files, as well as providing many other capabilities.

In our **requireJsLearning** project, we have three modules (files) which are not using AMD module format. These are person2, person3, and person4. In order for RequireJS to load such modules and make them available for usage by other modules, we need to provide some configuration settings.

If you look at config.js file in our project, you see the following code:

```
require.config({
    deps: ['main'],
    paths: {
    //'jquery' : 'libs/jquery'// if loading
    from local directory
        'person2': 'modules/person2', // location to
            none AMD modules
        'person3': 'modules/person3',
        'person4': 'modules/person4',
        'jquery': "https://code.jquery.com/jquery-1.12.3.min"
        // loading from CDN
    },
    shim: {
        "person2": {
            "exports": "person2"
                // use this alias in the global scope and
                pass it to modules as dependency
        },
        "person3": {
            deps: ['person4'],
            // none AMD module, depending on another
            non AMD module
            "exports": "person3"
        }
    }
});
```

Here, we are passing a configuration object to require.config method of RequireJS. The first property of this object defines main as a dependency (deps: ['main']). Remember that main module is the module that boots up our application, but in index.html file, we told RequireJS to load config.js using data-main attribute, as shown here:

```
<script  src="js/libs/require.js" data-main="js/config"></script>
```

When RequireJS loads config.js file, the configuration object is passed to require. config method. Then, RequireJS figures out that it needs to load main.js (by looking at the deps: ['main'] property on this object). Of course, in turn, by looking at the dependency list of main module, RequireJS loads all the dependencies for main module as well.

Setting paths in the config object

The next property set in the configuration object passed to `require.config` method is `paths` property. This property itself is an object and it's where we define the paths to our dependencies. For instance, see the following snippet:

```
'person2': 'modules/person2'
```

Here we tell RequireJS that, when it needs to load `person2`, it can find it in the `modules/person2.js` file. Remember that we do not provide the file extension for the file in this property.

Creating shims for non-AMD modules

The next property that we define in object passed to `require.config` method is `shim` property.

`shim` property is an object too and is used to provide configuration settings for non-AMD modules.

For instance, see how we are configuring `person3` module in the following code snippet:

```
"person3": {
            deps: ['person4'],
            // none AMD module, depending on another
            non AMD module
            "exports": "person3"
}
```

We tell RequireJS that, when you want to load `person3` module as a dependency, first you need to load `person4` (using `deps` property), and then let the consuming modules declare this module as a dependency using the keyword `person3`.

Consider how `stuff` module declares and consumes `person3` as a dependency in the following code snippet:

```
define(['person3'], function(person3) {
    console.log(person3.first +
        " --> Accessing person3.first from stuff");
    return {
        likes: ['Car', 'Bike', 'Scooter']
    };
});
```

In this way, we can load and consume non-AMD modules asynchronously, thanks to RequireJS.

To confirm that everything is working as it should and all the dependencies are resolved properly, we can load index.html in the browser. We should then see the following messages in the debugger tools console (I'm using Chrome browser):

```
Tim  --> Accessing person4 ; from person3
Sasan  --> Accessing person3.first from stuff
function (a,b){return new n.fn.init(a,b)}  --> Accessing jQuery from person
Accessing Person --> person first + person last; from main -> Sam SamLastName
function (a,b){return new n.fn.init(a,b)}  --> jquery from main
Accessing person2 --> person2.first ; from main -> Fay
```

I encourage you to have a look at the code related to this project (requireJsLearning) and use it to see how you can create, load, and consume modules using RequireJS.

For more in-depth information regarding this great library and the many different options that it provides, please visit http://requirejs.org/.

I hope this was a good introduction to AMD module format and RequireJS. Let's now use what we have learned from this section and re-factor our main application to load our modules the AMD way.

Refactoring Images Inc. application to use AMD format

To leverage the functionality that RequireJS provides for us, we are going to take two different approaches here. First, we are going to convert all of the submodules in the Core module into AMD modules.

Second, we are going to load all of our other files in the application, including our application's components, as non-AMD modules. These two approaches will provide us with a practical exercise to put our knowledge of RequireJS and AMD modules to good use.

Modifying Core submodules into AMD modules

In this section, we are going to look at ImagesInc_Core.LoggingHandler submodule and see how we can convert it into an AMD module. All the other submodules in the application can also be converted to AMD modules, following the same approach.

Consider how `ImagesInc_Core.LoggingHandler` submodule is implemented in our application:

```
ImagesInc_Core.LoggingHandler = (function(){

...


return {

        logMessage: self.logMessage,
        initialize: self.initialize
    };
})();
```

We were using an IIFE to return an object as a property on `ImagesInc_Core` global object (which is our MainCore module). This returned object is the interface to the code inside of our IIFE namespace.

To convert this submodule to an AMD module, we simply need to transfer the code which was originally inside the IIFE to `define` method provided to us by RequireJS.

Consider the following code snippet:

```
define(['MainCore'], function(ImagesInc_Core){
...

    return ImagesInc_Core.LoggingHandler = {

        logMessage: self.logMessage,
        initialize: self.initialize
    }

}
```

Notice that we are still returning an object from the callback function and we are also assigning it to `LoggingHandler` property of `ImagesInc_Core` object.

This approach allows us to easily convert our non-AMD submodules into AMD modules, with very little modification. This is mostly because, from the beginning, our architecture was designed to be a modular-based architecture. Now, thanks to RequireJS, we are able to load our submodule files asynchronously, without the need to add them as `<script>` tags to our `index.html` file.

Loading our non-AMD modules using RequireJS

We are going to load the rest of the files in our application, including MainCore, as non-AMD modules.

You may decide later on that you would like to convert these modules into AMD modules as well. I encourage you to do so, as it will be a valuable exercise. However, my goal here is to show you how AMD and non-AMD modules can work together in harmony, without much trouble at all.

As explained previously, to load non-AMD modules using RequireJS, we need to define them in `shim` property of our application's `config` file.

Remember that we load `config.js` file in our `index.html`, as shown here:

```
<script src="js/lib/require.js" data-main="js/config"></script>
```

`config.js` file in turn will cause the loading of our `main.js` file (as it has been defined as a dependency for `config.js` file), which does the bootstrapping of our application.

It is time for us to have a closer look at our application's `config.js` file.

Setting up our application's config.js file

Our application's `config.js` file consists of three main properties; `deps` property, which defines the dependencies of `config` file; `paths` property, which maps all of our dependencies to their physical file locations, and `shim` property, which is used to define the non-AMD modules in our application.

Have a look at `config` file, in the code snippet below:

```
require.config({
    deps: ['main'],
    paths:{
        'MainCore' : 'Modules/Core/MainCore',
        'Logger': 'Modules/Core/Logger',
        'AjaxEngine': 'Modules/Core/AjaxEngine',
        'CookieHandler': 'Modules/Core/CookieHandler',
        'NotificationHandler': 'Modules/Core/NotificationHandler',
        'StorageHandler': 'Modules/Core/StorageHandler',
        'Utilities': 'Modules/Core/Utilities',
        'SandBox' : 'Modules/SandBox/SandBox',
        'ImagesInc_Content': 'Components/ImagesInc_Content',
        'ImagesInc_Footer': 'Components/ImagesInc_Footer',
        'ImagesInc_Header': 'Components/ImagesInc_Header',
        'AppTester': 'Modules/AppTester/AppTester',
```

```
            'CookieHandlerTester':
                'Modules/AppTester/CookieHandlerTester',
            'StorageHandlerTester':
                'Modules/AppTester/StorageHandlerTester',
            'Base': 'Modules/Base/Base',
            'jquery': 'Modules/Base/jquery-1.10.2.min',
            'GlobalData_Sub': 'Modules/GlobalData/GlobalData_Sub',
            'GlobalData': 'Modules/GlobalData/GlobalData'
        },

    shim:{

        'Base':{
            exports : 'Base'
        },

        'jquery':{
            exports : 'jquery'

        },
    ...

    });
```

I think by now you are quite familiar with the types of configuration items that we set for our application in this file. Based on this configuration, RequireJS can now load our modules and files, asynchronously and in the correct order.

This implementation allows us to have a well-organized, maintainable, and scalable solution to loading our modules, without the need to list them all in our index.html file.

Booting up our application using RequireJS

Our main module is the module responsible for booting up our application.

Have a look at the following code snippet and see how this module is implemented:

```
// Application bootstrap file
var modulesToLoad = ['MainCore','Logger','AjaxEngine',
  'CookieHandler', 'NotificationHandler',
  'StorageHandler','Utilities','ImagesInc_Content',
   'ImagesInc_Footer', 'ImagesInc_Header','SandBox', 'AppTester',
  'CookieHandlerTester',
  'StorageHandlerTester', 'Base', 'jquery', 'GlobalData_Sub',
  'GlobalData'];
```

```
require(modulesToLoad, function(ImagesInc_Core, Logger,AjaxEngine,
    CookieHandler, NotificationHandler, StorageHandler, Utilities,
    ImagesInc_Content, ImagesInc_Footer, ImagesInc_Header, SandBox,
    Base, jquery, GlobalData_Sub, GlobalData){
    //register StorageHandler with MainCore
    ImagesInc_Core.StorageHandler.register = (function(){
    ImagesInc_Core.registerModule(ImagesInc_Core.StorageHandler);
    })();

    //add error handling to all methods of StorageHandler,
    in case localStorage not available
    if(ImagesInc_Core.Utilitizes){
    ImagesInc_Core.Utilitizes.addLocalStorageCheck(
    ImagesInc_Core.StorageHandler);
    }
    ImagesInc_Core.initializeAllModules();
    ImagesInc_Core.initializeAllComponents();
    ImagesInc_Core.handlePageChange(location.pathname);
});
```

As you can see, we have listed all of our application's dependencies in an array. Then, we have used `require` method to load them all and pass them to the callback function.

Inside this callback function, we execute the code necessary to get the application started up.

If you look at the **Network** tab of your browser's debugger tool (I use Chrome), you will see how RequireJS has loaded the necessary modules and files for our application, as shown in the following screenshot:

index.html	GET	200	document	Other
app.css	GET	304	stylesheet	index.html:8
require.js	GET	304	script	index.html:25
config.js	GET	304	script	require.js:34
main.js	GET	304	script	require.js:34
Logger.js	GET	304	script	require.js:34
AjaxEngine.js	GET	304	script	require.js:34
CookieHandler.js	GET	304	script	require.js:34
NotificationHandler.js	GET	304	script	require.js:34
StorageHandler.js	GET	304	script	require.js:34
Utilities.js	GET	304	script	require.js:34
SandBox.js	GET	304	script	require.js:34
Base.js	GET	304	script	require.js:34
GlobalData.js	GET	304	script	require.js:34

As you can see, modular architecture can help us greatly to manage our application pieces and their related dependencies with ease. I recommend that you spend some time exploring how to leverage the full functionality of AMD modules in your own applications.

CommonJS

As with AMD format, CommonJS (also known as CJS) is another format which defines JavaScript modules as objects that can be made available to any dependent code. CJS modules can only define objects, as opposed to AMD modules, which can define constructors and functions too.

Unlike AMD format, which takes a browser-first approach, CommonJS takes a server-first approach. It also covers a broader set of concerns which are server-related, such as io, file system, and alike.

Many developers (I'm one of them) use AMD format for browser-targeted modules and CommonJS for server-side targeted modules. However, you could use CJS format for browser modules as well.

Some of the tools that support CJS for the browsers are:

- **curl.js**: `http://github.com/unscriptable/curl`
- **SproutCore**: `http://sproutcore.com`

Let's have a look at a simple example to see how we can implement a CJS format module.

Implementing a CommonJS module

Imagine that we have a file called `moduleOne.js`. From inside this file, we can export a CJS module like so:

```
exports.someFunc = function(){

    return console.log("I am some function");
}
```

Here, `exports` is a global variable and contains the object which the module is making available to other modules that wish to consume it.

On the other hand, imagine that we have another module in `moduleTwo.js` file, which resides in the same directory as `moduleOne.js`.

moduleTwo can import moduleOne and consume it like so:

```
var firstModule = require('./moduleOne');
firstModule.someFunc();

exports.someApp = function(){
    return firstModule.someFunc();
}
exports.someOtherApp = function(){
    return console.log("I am some other app");
}
```

As you can see, in this module we use CJS require method to import the first module (someFunc), and then we can use it as firstModule.someFunc().

In moduleTwo.js, we are also exporting another module called someApp, which can be consumed by other modules in the application. Note that in the preceding example, we are in fact exporting more than one module from the same file.

Notice also that there is no define method to wrap our modules and return an object from the callback function, as opposed to what we saw in AMD format.

CJS syntax is similar to how ECMAScript 6 defines modules, and we will have a look at that in the next section.

For more information regarding CJS modules, please refer to the following resource online: http://www.commonjs.org/.

ECMAScript 6 modules

In the new version of JavaScript, **ECMAScript 6** (also known as **ES6**), native modules have been introduced. The following points are some of the most important aspects of these modules:

- Module code always automatically runs in strict mode
- Variables that are created in the top level of a module are not added to the global scope
- A module must export anything that should be available to the outside code
- A module can import bindings (things that are exported from other modules)

The main idea behind modules in ES6 is to give you complete control over what is accessible to the outside code from inside the module, as well as when the code inside of the module is executed.

Let's have a look at a simple example of an ES6 module.

Defining an ES6 module

We can define an ES6 module either inside of a .js file, or inside a <script> tag in our .html page.

Consider the following code snippet, from an imaginary simpleModule.js file:

```
var name = "Tom";
// export function
export function sayHello(name) {
    alert("Hello " + name);
}
function sayName(){
    alert('My name is: ' + name);
}
function sayBye(name) {
    alert("Bye " + name);
}
export sayBye;
```

In the preceding module, we have defined three functions as well as a module variable. Note that while the variable name is not inside of a function, its scope is still limited to the module. This means that no external code to the module can access it.

We have also used the keyword export to make two of our functions available to the potential consumers of the module. As you can see, we can use export either on the function declaration, as in the case of sayHello function, or as a reference, in the case of sayBye function.

To create a module as an embedded module in an .html file, we can use the following syntax:

```
<script type="module">
    var modulePrivateVar = 2
    alert("The value in the module is: " + modulePrivateVar);
</script>
```

Note that we have specified `type` of the script to be `module`, which causes the browser to treat the code inside the `<script>` tag as an ES6 module.

Consuming an ES6 module

When the external code to an ES6 module needs to have access to what has been exposed by the module, binding needs to be used.

Consider how we can get access to the two functions that were exposed by our first module, `simpleModule`, as shown here:

```
import { sayHello, sayBye } from "simpleModule.js";
sayHello();
sayBye();
sayName(); // error, sayName was not exported
```

As shown, we need to use the keyword `import` to create binding between the external code to the module and the functions that the module exports.

Also, notice that since `sayName` was not exported by the module, we have no access to it.

Module loading sequence in the browsers for ES6 modules

ES6 modules in the browsers are always loaded as soon as the browsers encounter the following tag:

```
<script type="module" src="simpleModule.js">
```

However, the code in the module is not executed until the document has been completely parsed.

Modules are also executed in the order in which they appear. This means that in our preceding examples, if we had listed our modules as:

```
<script type="module" src="simpleModule.js">
<script type="module">
    var modulePrivateVar = 2
    alert("The value in the module is: " + modulePrivateVar);
</script>
```

The code in `simpleModule.js` would be executed before the code for our embedded module would.

Since a module can also have its own dependencies, which it defines using the `import` statements (bindings), each module is parsed completely before its code is executed. This is so the dependencies can be resolved correctly.

This means, if the browser encounters an import statement in an already downloaded module, it will download the dependency first before executing the code in that module. This ensures that all the modules and their dependencies are loaded before any code-execution in the modules.

There is a lot more to ES6 modules than what we have covered here, as this was meant to be a very brief introduction. I encourage you to research the subject further on your own. There are many good resources online which you can refer to and I highly recommend the following sites for more information:

- `https://leanpub.com/understandinges6`
- `https://hacks.mozilla.org/2015/08/es6-in-depth-modules/`
- `https://developer.mozilla.org/en/docs/web/javascript/reference/statements/import`

Final note regarding our Images Inc. application

It is always a good idea to revisit and improve the quality of the code in our applications. As such, I have made some small modifications to the code-base related to this chapter. The latest project's code is a little more polished and linted. Also, I have made improvements to the visual responsiveness of the application in the browsers by making some changes to the related CSS files.

However, there are always things that can be improved further in any project and this application is no exception.

Nonetheless, I hope the application will provide a good starting point for your future projects.

Summary

As this was the last phase in the implementation of our application, in this chapter we discussed how we can improve the dependency management and loading of our modules in the browser.

By re-factoring our application's code, we converted our Core submodules to AMD modules and then used RequireJS to load all of our JavaScript files asynchronously from the server.

We saw how we can use RequireJS, which is mainly a script-loading library, to load our AMD and non-AMD modules.

We also covered different formats for defining modules in JavaScript and talked about AMD, CommonJS, and ES6 modules. Since this book is focused on using JavaScript in the browsers, we spent more time getting to know AMD modules, as they are better suited for this purpose.

In our overview of CommonJS and ES6 modules, we noted the similarities between the two formats and saw how ES6 modules can be used in our code.

I hope you have found this book informative and a good introduction to modular programming with JavaScript.

As always, there is a lot more to learn for all of us and I wish you great success in your future endeavors.

Index

www.ingramcontent.com/pod-product-compliance
Lightning Source LLC
Chambersburg PA
CBHW060530060326
40690CB00017B/3444